Praise

"This series provides a practical today." – John V. Biernacki, Partner, Jones Day

"*Inside the Minds* draws from the collective experience of the best professionals. The books are informative from an academic, and, more importantly, practical perspective. I highly recommend them." – Keith M. Aurzada, Partner, Bryan Cave LLP

"Aspatore's *Inside the Minds* series provides practical, cutting edge advice from those with insight into the real world challenges that confront businesses in the global economy." – Michael Bednarek, Partner, Shearman & Sterling LLP

"What to read when you want to be in the know—topical, current, practical, and useful information on areas of the law that everyone is talking about." – Erika L. Morabito, Partner, Patton Boggs LLP

"Some of the best insight around from sources in the know" – Donald R. Kirk, Shareholder, Fowler White Boggs PA

"The *Inside the Minds* series provides a unique window into the strategic thinking of key players in business and law." – John M. Sylvester, Partner, K&L Gates LLP

"Comprehensive analysis and strategies you won't find anywhere else." – Stephen C. Stapleton, Of Counsel, Dykema Gossett PLLC

"The *Inside the Minds* series is a real hands-on, practical resource for cutting edge issues." – Trey Monsour, Partner, Haynes and Boone LLP

"A tremendous resource, amalgamating commentary from leading professionals that is presented in a concise, easy to read format." – Alan H. Aronson, Shareholder, Akerman Senterfitt

"Unique and invaluable opportunity to gain insight into the minds of experienced professionals." – Jura C. Zibas, Partner, Lewis Brisbois Bisgaard & Smith LLP

"A refreshing collection of strategic insights, not dreary commonplaces, from some of the best of the profession." – Roger J. Magnuson, Partner, Dorsey & Whitney LLP

"Provides valuable insights by experienced practitioners into practical and theoretical developments in today's ever-changing legal world." – Elizabeth Gray, Partner, Willkie, Farr & Gallagher LLP

"This series provides invaluable insight into the practical experiences of lawyers in the trenches." – Thomas H. Christopher, Partner, Kilpatrick Stockton LLP

ASPATORE

Aspatore Books, a Thomson Reuters business, exclusively publishes C-Level executives and partners from the world's most respected companies and law firms. Each publication provides professionals of all levels with proven business and legal intelligence from industry insiders—direct and unfiltered insight from those who know it best. Aspatore Books is committed to publishing an innovative line of business and legal titles that lay forth principles and offer insights that can have a direct financial impact on the reader's business objectives.

Each chapter in the *Inside the Minds* series offers thought leadership and expert analysis on an industry, profession, or topic, providing a future-oriented perspective and proven strategies for success. Each author has been selected based on their experience and C-Level standing within the business and legal communities. *Inside the Minds* was conceived to give a first-hand look into the leading minds of top business executives and lawyers worldwide, presenting an unprecedented collection of views on various industries and professions.

INSIDE THE MINDS

Structuring Commercial Real Estate Transactions

Leading Lawyers on Facilitating Successful Deals and Contracts That Meet Client Needs

ASPATORE

©2011 Thomson Reuters/Aspatore
All rights reserved. Printed in the United States of America.

Inside the Minds Project Manager, Tiffany Smith; edited by Michaela Falls; proofread by Melanie Zimmerman

No part of this publication may be reproduced or distributed in any form or by any means, or stored in a database or retrieval system, except as permitted under Sections 107 or 108 of the U.S. Copyright Act, without prior written permission of the publisher. This book is printed on acid-free paper.

Material in this book is for educational purposes only. This book is sold with the understanding that neither any of the authors nor the publisher is engaged in rendering legal, accounting, investment, or any other professional service as a part of this book. Neither the publisher nor the authors assume any liability for any errors or omissions or for how this book or its contents are used or interpreted or for any consequences resulting directly or indirectly from the use of this book. For legal advice or any other, please consult your personal lawyer or the appropriate professional.

The views expressed by the individuals in this book (or the individuals on the cover) do not necessarily reflect the views shared by the companies they are employed by (or the companies mentioned in this book). The employment status and affiliations of authors with the companies referenced are subject to change.

Aspatore books may be purchased for educational, business, or sales promotional use. For information, please e-mail West.customer.service@thomson.com.

ISBN 978-0-314-27803-6

For corrections, updates, comments or any other inquiries please e-mail TLR.AspatoreEditorial@thomson.com.

First Printing, 2011
10 9 8 7 6 5 4 3 2 1

Mat #41191561

Contents

Shari B. Olefson   7
Shareholder, **Fowler White Boggs PA**
THE REALITIES OF PRACTICING COMMERCIAL
REAL ESTATE TRANSACTION LAW TODAY

Joel D. Rubin   27
Partner and Co-Chair, Institutional Real Estate Group,
Seyfarth Shaw LLP
UNDERSTANDING THE COMPLEXITIES OF THE
REAL ESTATE TRANSACTION PROCESS

Alfred M. Meyerson   37
Partner, **Thompson & Knight LLP**
PRACTICAL ASPECTS OF COMMERCIAL REAL
ESTATE TRANSACTIONS

Kevin J. Connolly   47
Shareholder, **Anderson Kill & Olick PC**
LEGAL ISSUES ASSOCIATED WITH
INTEGRATED CONSTRUCTION CONTRACTING

Jane B. Morgan   63
Member, **Watkins & Eager PLLC**
TACTICS FOR FACILITATING SUCCESSFUL REAL
ESTATE TRANSACTIONS

Kwame A. Benjamin   83
Partner, **Seyfarth Shaw LLP**
IMPLEMENTING SUCCESSFUL COMMERCIAL
REAL ESTATE STRATEGIES

Dennis M. Horn 97
Partner and Co-Chair, District of Columbia Practice Group,
Holland & Knight LLP
ARE WE HEADED INTO "SEVEN FAT YEARS"?:
WHAT REAL ESTATE LAWYERS CAN EXPECT
FOR THE FUTURE

Appendices 109

The Realities of Practicing Commercial Real Estate Transaction Law Today

Shari B. Olefson
Shareholder
Fowler White Boggs PA

ASPATORE

Introduction

My practice started in the late 1980s, around the same time that the Resolution Trust Corporation (RTC) was shutting down so many S&Ls and taking over a number of the properties those S&Ls had financed. An outsider might think that today's situation with the FDIC taking over banks and the need to work through so many of those now defunct commercial real estate credits is similar to the RTC days, but it is very different. That's primarily because, the last time around, commercial real estate (CRE) assets were, for the most part, liquid. Now, in the majority of cases, they are not. Instead, many commercial projects are often under water, so the approach and strategy, from both a business and a legal perspective, need to be very different too. Back then, our marching orders, as commercial real estate litigators and transactional experts, would have been to get our hands on the title to those CRE properties as quickly as possible so that the bank could sell them and satisfy the debts. Today, the banks know that selling CRE properties may be difficult, and if it can be done, in many cases the proceeds will not be sufficient to pay off the entire obligations so, contrary to the good old days, that will not be the end of it. Instead, we'll be pursuing guarantors or taking a haircut, both expensive propositions. This backdrop is important to any attorney considering a CRE practice today because it affects every deal that's happening. For that reason, understanding today's environment and dynamics is essential. Clearly, there is an infinite variety of CRE transaction types and sizes and a likewise varied range of experience and expertise among CRE practitioners. For purposes of this discussion, we will focus on practitioners familiar with real estate, but not necessarily commercial real estate, and considering starting a CRE transactional practice representing average investors in today's new environment.

The Parties Involved in Today's CRE Transactions

Much of the commercial real estate that is being purchased now is not being purchased directly from a typical seller-owner who is in good financial condition, as has traditionally been the case. In the past, it was not unusual to have multiple offers on a property, including offers above the asking price. Sellers were driving the proverbial boat. That is obviously not occurring today. Most financially healthy sellers are waiting the market out rather than listing their CRE property for sale now because the general assumption today is, if you're selling you're in trouble. This dilemma is having a significant impact on the broader CRE environment and likely exacerbating the duration of time it will likely take before the CRE market recovers.

For these and other reasons, buying distressed assets has become the predominant commercial real estate transaction. If you plan to start a CRE practice today, it is highly likely that you will end up talking to a seller who has his or her back up against the wall or to a bank that owns the property and, in either case, the parties will be operating under a different set of dynamics than in prior years when the CRE deals involved more traditional sellers. In either case, the rules have changed. The seller is no longer in the driver's seat. The buyer has a lot more leverage now. You'll quickly find that when dealing with banks, both the representatives you deal with and the banks' internal processes (including the processes that most banks utilize to approve purchase offer contracts and closing documents like the settlement statement and net proceeds that will be paid to the bank), have a noticeable impact on the CRE deals themselves. Depending upon how they are managed, special assets officers at banks can be as much a part of the problem as they are part of the solution. Because of the need at many banks to ramp up and handle large volumes of distressed CRE assets quickly, and the sudden needs that acquiring another bank can create, many special assets officers are "newbies." Even though they are positioned as the point people for these CRE transactions, there is seldom such a thing as a single person who can independently approve purchase offer contracts and the like, for example, at a bank. At a minimum, two or three signatures are required, if not full committee approval. With regard to this specific example, it's advisable to always ask anyone who says he or she will "get back to you" with a response (for example, on a short sale offer) exactly what the approval process and timeline for getting that answer is so that you can manage client (and everyone else's) expectations. And the necessity of waiting for these types of approvals from bank committees that may, for example, meet only once a month, needs to be taken into account when drafting purchase offer contract acceptance deadlines. Banks do the best they can, but dealing with a bank is never the same as dealing with someone who is an actual owner-seller and has his or her own personal pocketbook on the line.

The Real Reasons CRE Assets are Beginning to Trade Again

CRE prices are beginning to adjust to a point where buyers and sellers can make a deal as the banks write down bad CRE credits, become able to sell those assets, and prices find a bottom to climb from. For those not familiar with the anatomy of a CRE credit write down, in a nutshell, cap rates, or the values for these properties, fell so low over the past few years due to reduced tenants and rent rates that the owners either could not cover their debt service and other expenses or could not refinance when their loans matured and fell into default. Initially, banks tried to avoid reflecting these value drops and imminent defaults on their books since reflecting these issues in accounting then requires the banks to add sufficient coverage funds into their capital reserves. Likewise, selling an asset for less than what is owed, even if the lesser amount is actual current market value, requires a credit write down and is one of the reasons CRE assets have not been trading. But again, over the last year or so, banks have had no choice but to write down the value of CRE assets which then allows the credits and underlying assets to be dealt with. And, of course, those banks that have taken over others under FDIC Loss Share Agreements can reflect the lower CRE assets and credit value with less challenges since this risk is generally reflected in the bank acquisition price.

Current CRE Value and Pricing Influences

When values plummeted in commercial real estate, all project types were affected, from hotels and resorts to offices and industrial warehouses. The CRE properties that are starting to recover first are multi-family projects. These assets are recovering faster because there are users for them (i.e., residential tenants) since so many folks are hesitant to buy a home now due to uncertainly in the residential sector. Still, others are unable to buy due to poor credit, tighter lending, or a recent foreclosure. As folks are losing their homes to foreclosure, or renters are reluctant to get into the market and buy a house, renting as a housing option has become more popular. There is an increasing ability to fill these residential rental units, and the lease terms tend to be shorter on a rental unit than for a warehouse or other commercial property mean that investors can increase the rents more readily. We can expect to see increases in residential rental rates to justify these acquisition prices. Hopefully, increasing residential rents will eventually drive folks back into housing purchases and absorption of the surplus residential inventory. Fannie Mae and Freddie Mac have always been notable players in financing multi-family CRE projects. The fact that these GSEs are still lending and financing from traditional banks for other categories of CRE investments has been scarce is also helping to keep up multi-family sector values and prices for most other types of CRE projects today, lenders will consider financing only solid owner-occupied projects with a decent down payment. In some areas, the sales prices of multi-family rental properties have increased from $30 a unit to $50 a unit.

In hotel, industrial, and office, sellers are recognizing that they cannot get the high prices they'd previously grown accustomed to anymore, but even realistic prices for those assets may not be enough to bring buyers back into the market. Who wants to carry an office building if there are no tenants to put in it? Industrial and retail properties, of course, mirror what is happening in the economy. Manufacturers and exporters will do well in the coming years thanks to the devalued dollar. So we can expect warehouses, for example, that service those types of companies to increase in value. Hospitality properties, especially the higher-end properties in gateway business-oriented cities, seem to be doing well because hotel rooms can be re-priced on a daily basis.

Because these CRE assets are taking so long to price right, there is much pent up money on the sidelines. CRE purchasers are on every fund's radar screen. The annual Association of Foreign Investors in Real Estate Investors survey indicated strong global interest in US CRE: "The weak dollar represents two opportunities for foreign capital. First, the weak dollar allows more property purchased per foreign currency unit…when the dollar rebounds, the investment value increases again, making the real estate investment doubly attractive to foreigners. Current currency prices avail the foreign investor an eighteen to forty-six percent discount for US assets compared to foreign markets including Europe and Asia. Currently, foreign investors own $70 billion worth of US commercial real estate assets (approximately 3.1 percent of the total inventory by market value), according to AFIRE (Association of Foreign Investors in Real Estate)." Foreign investors have increased their intent to purchase in the United States 60 percent over last year. When working with foreign investors, other issues may be relevant to the CRE practitioner, which are beyond the scope of this discussion. This is one of the reasons we're seeing CRE prices, again on multi-family in particular, growing as investors outbid each other with money they simply have to deploy.

Because increased foreign investment in CRE is anticipated, it behooves the CRE transaction practitioner to be familiar with some of the tax, immigration, and regulatory issues that could potentially affect foreign investment in US CRE.

Decline in Foreclosure Actions on Commercial Real Estate Credits

We are seeing fewer CRE defaults because, again, banks are increasingly motivated and able to work out pending and actual defaults with commercial property owners, borrowers, and buyers. We're seeing far more short sales and, even if modifications are not consistent with the desire to get out of a credit or meet FDIC Loss Share Agreement deadlines, banks are at least more frequently willing to consider forbearances now if there is a near-future opportunity for an exit strategy. Even as the economy improves and CRE asset prices begin to do the same, we are likely going to continue to see some defaults and foreclosures. This is primarily because CRE credit is, and will likely remain, tight for some time. As the loans on value deflated CRE assets mature, it is often impossible for the owner-borrowers to refinance.

Today's Environment Dictates CRE Transaction Structure

In terms of how CRE transactions are being structured today, one strategy we're seeing more frequently is note purchases. This is a result of the current environmental dynamics we've discussed and long foreclosure backlogs. Acquiring commercial real estate assets by buying the note involves added risk to the investor-client. In some cases, the note is purchased with the intent to get paid off. In other cases, the investor-client's intent is to eventually own the underlying property. In either case, the same due diligence that would normally be done by the legal practitioner on a traditional CRE asset purchase is appropriate. Unfortunately, under these circumstances borrower-owners may be unaware of the sale by the bank or uncooperative. As an attorney for a CRE market buyer, the best case, of course, is one where the owner of that property or at least a manager familiar with it is around and will be cooperative and involved in the ownership transition. But again, today's reality is that access to the property may be impractical or impossible, necessitating heavy reliance on documentation that the bank has on file. If the property is listed with a realtor, access in a more covert manner may be the only option. These and other similar realities are relevant to and need to be contemplated by the CRE transactional practitioner when drafting, negotiating, and reviewing CRE purchase offer contracts in today's new environment.

The second major risk in note purchases is, of course, the risk of prepayment or default, both of which can be priced into the deal structure itself. If the note is already in default, waiting for the borrower to file a response or "answer" to the lawsuit complaint may mitigate some of that risk. The answer, of course, provides insight into what the borrower thinks his or her defenses and counterclaims to the foreclosure action are going to be. In addition to buying the potential for any income stream from the note or the potential to one day foreclose and own the underlying commercial real estate, note purchasers unfortunately are also buying the potential to become embroiled in a lawsuit with the borrower. A note purchaser essentially steps into the shoes of lender, but may have little idea what the lender may or may not have done to create defenses or counterclaims. Particularly in today's anti-bank political and legal climate, and high incidence of borrowers filing bankruptcy, commercial real estate transactions structured as note purchases should incorporate appropriate representations, warranties, and indemnifications from the selling note holder, and, of course, factor the legal and time costs into the purchase price. In some cases it may be appropriate to negotiate for conflicts to be waived and bank's counsel to complete the foreclosure action for a pre-negotiated fee. Needless to say, high likelihood of a summary judgment increases the probability that this type of arrangement can be negotiated.

The Role of the Attorney in Structuring Commercial Real Estate Transactions

Defining the Scope of Representation

The attorney's role in structuring CRE transactions varies widely depending on the deal itself and the client. The initial attorney-client meeting will typically establish more precisely what the scope of representation in a particular deal will be. Getting a clear picture of the client's potential pitfalls and concerns, especially those regarding tax issues, partnership understandings and dynamics, entity structure, liabilities, timelines, contingencies, lender requirements, due diligence, and other deal specific issues related to the CRE project and seller at hand, at the initial client meeting is essential in order to ensure that client expectations and transaction fundamentals are properly met. Clarifying the identity and role(s) of each professional who will be involved in the CRE transaction will help the practitioner to avoid confusion and potential mishap. For example, oftentimes even the most basic CRE deal involves one or more real estate broker. Clarifying his or her role and the chain of command and communication at the initial client meeting will prove beneficial for all.

Structuring Commercial Real Estate Transaction Holding Entities

Generally speaking, the structure of a commercial real estate holding entity is designed to create a degree of certainty and predictability. In the past, lender financing requirements often drove CRE holding entity structure. Today, in an environment more skewed toward cash transactions, CRE holding entity structure is more heavily driven by tax and business or operational factors. And in some cases, more than one separate entity may still be appropriate. For example, for a hotel project, a separate operating company entity and a separate holding company entity for the commercial real estate asset itself may be appropriate for business liability and other reasons. And, establishing a separate holding entity of each CRE asset is still advisable for many of the same reasons. Average CRE investors today often utilize a limited liability company (LLC) holding entity structure, but the use of trusts, corporations (both Subchapter S and C), limited partnerships, general partnerships, or combinations involving layered holding entity structures are not uncommon. The transaction dollar size, complexity, players, potential liabilities, and other project-specific factors have always had, and still do have, the most significant impact on the holding entity structure for a specific CRE transaction. LLCs still tend to be the favored holding entity structure for average CRE investors today, primarily because of the tax benefits and liability protection.

The same legal guidance that has always applied to maintaining business entity integrity still applies to CRE holding entities as well, in order to minimize the risk of a court disregarding the CRE holding entity, or "piercing the corporate veil." In making these determinations, courts will look to traditional indicators like CRE holding entities that are improperly or undercapitalized or co-mingling funds between holding entities and individuals.

Fundamental Components of a Commercial Real Estate Purchase Offer Contract

Some CRE transactions will land on the practitioner's desk after the purchase offer contract has been signed. Other times counsel will be central in drafting, reviewing, and perhaps even negotiating the CRE purchase offer contract. Likewise, counsel may or may not be expected to participate in CRE transaction, financial analysis, and financing discussions, or document preparation or review and negotiation, all of which is, again, best established when the scope of representation is first addressed at the initial client meeting. But even in those cases where the scope of representation does not extend to involvement with the financial analysis or financing of a CRE acquisition, for example, it is beneficial for the CRE practitioner to understand these various transaction aspects as they relate to the CRE purchase offer contract, due diligence, and overseeing the deal itself. As is the case with any real estate purchase offer contract, CRE purchase offer contracts typically incorporate a description of the real property being sold, the purchase price, the good faith escrow deposit, defaults and remedies, and contingencies to the transaction closing (typically financing and due diligence), and seller warranties and representations. The exact scope of due diligence for a particular CRE transaction will depend upon the type of project specifics and negotiation leverage between the parties. For example, in the case of a non-owner occupied CRE transaction, the asset, cap rate, and value are directly correlated to the income stream and the lease that produced that income stream. Accordingly, a comprehensive review of those leases will typically be a central component of the due diligence conducted in connection with the purchase of that type of CRE asset. For a vacant land or CRE construction project acquisition, a comprehensive review of the construction contracts and entitlements might be key. In still other transactions, permits, licenses, and service contracts may be central to the due diligence. A sample CRE purchase offer contract is included as Appendix B.

Acceptable purchase offer contract contingencies and time frames for completing them traditionally vary over time depending on the market dynamics and which party (i.e., the buyer, seller or, in today's environment, lender) has the most leverage in a particular CRE transaction. In today's market, buyers tend to have the leverage over sellers, but the banks have the leverage over everyone. In transactions where the seller will be providing information essential for due diligence, it is wise to start the due diligence time period clock ticking after the seller has provided the last of the due diligence materials needed for the buyer to begin his or her review. It is not unusual for a buyer to initially agree to a due diligence period dictated by the lender or seller in the purchase offer contract, with the intent to demand an extension of the due diligence time period or other purchase offer contract concessions (for example, a price reduction) once the transaction is under contract and well underway. But generally, in today's CRE market, and particularly with distressed assets, purchase prices are being discounted so much that the deals are "as is" and extensive contingencies or due diligence periods won't fly.

The CRE Transaction Closing Checklist and Critical Dates Schedule

Following the initial client meeting and receipt of a signed purchase offer contract, preparation of a comprehensive CRE transaction closing checklist, reflecting who will be providing each item, is an important next step. It is not unusual for closing checklists to evolve with the transaction. Accordingly, it is advisable to periodically revisit this document and consider it a "work in progress."

Preparation of a CRE transaction critical dates schedule is also helpful in avoiding potential problems. Preparing a preliminary CRE transactional critical dates schedule while the purchase offer contract is still being negotiated or reviewed enables practitioners to anticipate and flesh out potential timing issues while they can still be avoided. And asking all parties to approve the final version of the CRE transaction critical dates schedule will ensure that everyone is on the same page, at least where the transaction deadline expectations are concerned. A sample CRE transaction critical dates schedule is included as Appendix A.

CRE Transaction Closing Documents

Real estate transaction practitioners familiar with closing residential real estate transactions will find that the closing documents for CRE transactions are very similar. The primary differences between documents for a CRE transaction closing and a residential real estate closing are:

CRE deals are not governed by the Real Estate Settlement Procedures Act (RESPA). Accordingly, the various disclosures and documents required under RESPA are not necessary.

The threshold for seller liability in connection with a CRE transaction is lower than it is for sellers in residential transactions (for example, under *Johnson v. Davis*). Instead, caveat emptor is more prevalent. Accordingly, the purchase offer contract representations and warranties negotiated in a particular CRE transaction tend to be more deal specific. Likewise, the potential issues in connection with a CRE transaction (for example, hazardous waste) tend to be more significant than, say, an undisclosed roof leak one might encounter in connection with an undisclosed defect on a residential transaction.

Because the use of holding entities is more common in CRE transactions than it is in residential deals, the use of personal guaranties by lenders is more common, and holding entity-related documents, such as evidence of good standing, authorization, and resolutions, will be needed, often from both sellers and buyers.

Because the CRE assets themselves tend to be more complicated and have more "moving parts" than a typical residential property (for example, leases, inventory, permits, etc.), CRE transactions tend to involve more due diligence and more documentation addressing those moving parts such as UCC-1, Financing Statements, and an Assignments of Leases, Rents and Profits.

The following is a short list of the basic documents typically utilized at a CRE transaction closing:

Seller/Buyer

    1. Deed
    2. Bill of Sale
    3. Seller's Affidavit
    4. Assignment and Assumption Agreement (i.e., leases, contracts, licenses, permits, warranties, guarantees, insurances, etc.)
    5. Entity Operating Agreements, authorizations, and evidence of good standing
    6. Settlement or Closing Statement

Borrower/Lender

    1. Promissory Note
    2. Mortgage
    3. Personal Guaranty
    4. Loan Agreement
    5. Assignment of Leases, Rents, and Profits
    6. UCC-1 Financing Statements
    7. Environmental Indemnity
    8. Opinion of Borrower's Counsel

Seller representations and warranties, borrower guaranties, and counsel's opinion letters are typically the most highly negotiated documents. Again, this discussion is for the purposes of an entry level CRE transaction practitioner on the buyer-borrower transaction side. One example of a negotiation stance borrower's counsel will likely encounter today (as opposed to in prior years) is lenders requesting a guaranty only from the financially strongest party in the borrower's camp, as opposed to guarantees from each individual. This is one result of the many cases lenders have recently faced involving multiple guarantors on defaulted credits with each hiding behind or pointing the finger toward the other guarantors.

The documents used in connection with a typical CRE transaction note purchase (as previously discussed) include:

    1. Allonge
    2. Assignment of Mortgage
    3. Representations and Warranties (and sometimes Indemnification)

Examples of each of these documents are included as Appendices C, E, and F. In completing a CRE note purchase, the underlying loan documents, collateral title, and pleadings should be carefully reviewed. With all of the recent issues involving "holder in due course," if a note has been previously assigned verifying that all prior conveyances were properly documented and that the note seller has the original loan documents is essential.

Common Commercial Real Estate Transaction Mishaps

Some of the more common mishaps encountered by CRE transaction counsel tend to arise from poor communication and general oversight. Again, fleshing out the potential issues proactively, clearly establishing expectations in terms of scope of representation, communicating the specific role each professional will be playing (i.e., who will be doing what, who has what authority, and the chain of command and communication), and then documenting all of this in a comprehensive CRE transaction closing checklist and CRE transaction critical dates schedule will avoid the lion's share of potential mishaps. Whenever possible, eliminating nonessential folks from the middle of more common communications is also advisable. For example, calling one person to ask if he or she has heard back from another person is a red flag that folks are unnecessarily being put in the middle and miscommunication and delay are adding otherwise avoidable risk. Other areas to be aware of are discussed in the next section.

Some Relevant Commercial Real Estate Legal Issues, Case Law, and Statutory Considerations

Reflective of the CRE market itself, the legal issues, case law, and statutory considerations most relevant to commercial real estate transactions today relate to circumstances arising from the real estate boom and bust and the abundance of CRE distressed assets in inventory as opposed to the more traditional "caveat emptor" and similar commercial real estate legal issues.

Successor Liability

Successor developer liability (i.e., for example with regard to construction defects, lienors, and homeowner or condominium associations) has been front and center. Liability of this nature is still inhibiting both lender and buyer willingness to step into certain sectors of CRE assets. Risk aversion to these unknowns is always an issue, but in today's CRE transaction environment, it is a factor for more assets than before and is, accordingly, having a bigger impact on the overall CRE market than before.

To encourage banks to move forward with CRE foreclosures where necessary (many banks have been delaying CRE foreclosures on certain assets due to uncertainty in terms of the liabilities they would be taking on, if they acquire title to the CRE assets) and the trading of these CRE assets, several states have amended their respective statutes. In many cases, as case law has further carved out, states have tweaked and clarified definitions (for example, the statutory definition of who will and will not be considered a "successor developer") and responsibilities (for example, for HOA fees or to contract purchasers for misappropriated deposits or defaults). On a side note, the Chinese drywall lawsuits have further complicated the impact of successor liability by adding this new risk and the significant dollar amount associated with it into the mix.

Individual Unit Purchaser Contract and Deposit Rights

Another area that has been fraught with recent challenges involves distressed CRE assets involving individual unit purchasers, such as condominium development projects. CRE investors in these projects often step into the shoes of seller-developers in the resale of the underlying individual units to contract purchasers. The rights of purchasers under these contracts and, in particular, their rights to the refund of good faith deposit funds, which may have already been utilized by the original developer, is a legal area that CRE transaction practitioners are encountering with significantly more frequency than before.

Title and Encumbrance Related Issues

Another nuance we didn't see so much the last time around is more title related. During the boom real estate years, several states, including Florida, invented creative ways to help developers subsidize commercial real estate development. One such mechanism is special taxing districts, known as CDDs. CDDs essentially enabled developers to pass on financial responsibility for paying for infrastructure to future individual unit owners within a development. When the CRE market first crashed, many banks and CRE buyers were surprised to find that their equity positions were subject to these expensive prior lienors issues.

CRE Development Entitlements

It is not uncommon for CRE developers to agree to the payment of significant development impact fees over time, most of which are tied to the granting of development entitlements. These CRE project lenders and buyers are now faced with the prospect of having to pay or renegotiate these fees and their payment and other deadlines (such as the deadline to pull permits or begin construction) or lose the development entitlements. Without development entitlements, many CRE assets are virtually worthless, or certainly worth less than they are with the development entitlements in place. What's more, lest we forget, many local governments are experiencing their own budgetary issues and may see deep-pocket CRE development project buyers as a potential solution, particularly those requesting not only development entitlement time extensions, but also other changes to the project's development entitlements (for example, changes in the project design, use, or density). These types of added cost and liability are typically priced into the CRE transaction deal and entitlement related time frames carefully monitored by counsel.

Holder in Due Course Status

Whether a CRE transaction is structured as a traditional asset purchase or a note purchase, holder in due course is a potential issue with a plethora of still-evolving case law and political hot potatoes surrounding it. The now infamous "robo-signers" (clerical workers at large, high volume foreclosure law firms, commonly referred to as "mills," who violated state and federal foreclosure laws in many cases by filing flawed affidavits, including those "robo-signed," to have been true and accurate without actually having been reviewed) seems to have skewed courts against lenders in those cases where the actual holder in due course of a note is in question. Accordingly, it is prudent for the CRE transaction practitioner to include in CRE transaction due diligence additional vigilance in confirming: (a) in the case of a traditional distressed CRE asset purchase, that the foreclosure was properly done and that the foreclosing lender was in fact the proper note holder to have been foreclosing in the first place, and (b) in the case of a note purchase, that the lender the note is being purchased from is indeed the proper holder of that note.

Conclusion

I believe that the next few years will be filled with unhappy endings to many investor and lender CRE investment stories, each of which presents an opportunity for new buyers and for their CRE transaction attorneys.

Key Takeaways

- Buying distressed assets has become the predominant commercial real estate transaction. Banks are often in the driver's seat
- The necessity of waiting for approvals from bank committees that may, for example, meet only once a month, needs to be taken into account when drafting purchase offer contract acceptance deadlines.
- Selling an asset for less than what is owed, even if the lesser amount is actual current market value, requires a credit write down by the bank and is one of the reasons CRE assets have not been trading. Over the last year or so, banks have had no choice but to write down the value of CRE assets, which then allows the credits and underlying assets to be dealt with. Those banks that have taken over others under FDIC Loss Share Agreements can reflect the lower CRE assets and credit value with less challenges since this risk is generally reflected in the bank acquisition price.
- The CRE properties that are starting to recover first are multi-family projects because there are users for them (i.e., residential tenants) since so many folks are hesitant to buy a home now due to uncertainly in the residential sector. Still others are unable to buy due to poor credit, tighter lending, or a recent foreclosure. Lease terms tend to be shorter on a residential rental unit than for a warehouse or other commercial property mean that investors can increase the rents more. The fact that these GSEs are still lending, and financing from traditional banks for other categories of CRE investments has been scarce, is also helping to keep up multi-family sector values and prices. For most other types of CRE projects

today, lenders will consider financing only solid owner-occupied projects with a decent down payment.
- Manufacturers and exporters will do well in the coming years thanks to the devalued dollar. This will help the industrial and warehouse sector.
- Hospitality properties, especially the higher-end properties in gateway business-oriented cities, seem to be doing well in part because hotel rooms can be re-priced on a daily basis.
- There is much pent up investor money on the sidelines and the weak dollar represents two opportunities for foreign capital.
- Even as the economy improves and CRE asset prices begin to do the same, we are likely going to continue to see some defaults and foreclosures. This is primarily because CRE credit is, and will likely remain, tight for some time. As the loans on value deflated CRE assets mature, it is often impossible for the owner-borrowers to refinance.
- One strategy we're seeing more frequently is note purchases.
- Acquiring commercial real estate assets by buying the note involves added risk to the investor-client.
- If the note is already in default, waiting for the borrower to file a response or "answer" to the lawsuit complaint may mitigate some of that risk.
- Particularly in today's anti-bank political and legal climate, and high incidence of borrower's filing bankruptcy, commercial real estate transactions structured as note purchases should incorporate appropriate representations, warranties, and indemnifications from the selling note holder (particularly regarding holder in due course status), and, of course, factor the legal and time costs into the purchase price.
- Getting a clear picture of the client's potential pitfalls and concerns, especially those regarding tax issues, partnership understandings and dynamics, entity structure, liabilities, timelines, contingencies, lender requirements, due diligence, and other deal specific issues related to the CRE project and seller at hand at the initial client meeting is essential in order to ensure that client expectations and transaction fundamentals are properly met.

- In some cases, more than one separate business entity may be appropriate. Average CRE investors today often utilize a limited liability company (LLC) holding entity structure, but the use of trusts, corporations (both Subchapter S and C), limited partnerships, general partnerships, or combinations involving layered holding entity structures are not uncommon. Establishing a separate holding entity of each CRE asset is still advisable. The transaction dollar size, complexity, players, potential liabilities, and other project-specific factors have always had, and still do have, the most significant impact on the holding entity structure for a specific CRE transaction.
- It is not unusual for closing checklists to evolve with the transaction. Accordingly, it is advisable to periodically revisit this document and consider it a "work in progress."
- Preparing a preliminary CRE transaction critical dates schedule while the purchase offer contract is still being negotiated or reviewed enables practitioners to anticipate and flesh out potential timing issues while they can still be avoided. Asking all parties to approve the final version of the CRE transaction critical dates schedule will ensure that everyone is on the same page.
- CRE transactions are not governed by the Real Estate Settlement Procedures Act (RESPA). Accordingly, the various disclosures and documents required under RESPA are not necessary.
- The threshold for seller liability in connection with a CRE transaction is lower than it is for sellers in residential transactions (for example, under *Johnson v. Davis*). Instead, caveat emptor is more prevalent. Accordingly, the purchase offer contract representations and warranties negotiated in a particular CRE transaction tend to be more deal specific.
- Because title to most CRE projects is held in an entity, as opposed to individually, the use of personal guaranties by lenders is common, and holding entity-related documents will be needed.
- CRE transactions tend to involve more due diligence and more documentation addressing the many "moving parts" of many CRE assets.
- Successor developer liability has been front and center in CRE investing over the past few years.

- When the CRE market first crashed, many banks and CRE buyers were surprised to find that their equity positions were subject to heretofore seldom encountered expensive prior lienor issues like CDDs.
- Many CRE project lenders and buyers are now faced with the prospect of having to contend with or renegotiate impact and other development entitlement fees and deadlines or lose the development entitlements and the asset value they add.
- Whether a CRE transaction is structured as a traditional asset purchase or a note purchase, holder in due course is a potential issue with a plethora of still-evolving case law and political hot potatoes surrounding it.

Related Resources

- Meredith Freeman, *Real Estate Case Summaries*, ActionLine. Spring 2010, page 31
- SHARI B. OLEFSON, FORECLOSURE NATION: Mortgaging the American Dream (Prometheus Books, NY (2009) www.foreclosurenationthebook.com
- http://www.afire.org/foreign_data/2010/2.shtm

Shari B. Olefson, a shareholder at Fowler White Boggs P.A, is one of only a handful of lawyers who is a bar certified real estate attorney and has earned a master of law degree in real property, land development, and finance. As the former CEO of a Fortune 300 joint venture title insurance company, Ms. Olefson brings common sense practicality, business acumen, clear thinking, and entrepreneurship to every matter she handles.

Licensed to practice in New York, Washington, DC, and Florida since 1989, her practice has focused on real estate and business transactions for domestic and international investors, lenders and developers, and resolving the disputes that sometimes result from transactions and business relationships, including complex business and real estate mediation, workouts, and foreclosures. Ms. Olefson is highly experienced with all asset types including retail, office, industrial, multi-family and custom residential, shopping centers, restaurants, out-parcels, marinas, hotel-motel, mixed use, raw land, receivables, inventory, and stock. Ms. Olefson's business background includes all facets of entity selection and structure, including syndication, participation, joint ventures, and mergers and acquisitions.

Ms. Olefson has also represented lending and investment institutions creating credit programs and structuring and restructuring loan portfolios and commercial transactions. In addition to being a renowned attorney and remarkably intuitive businesswoman, Ms. Olefson is a highly experienced journalist, news commentator, author-educator, speaker, and Supreme Court certified mediator, with a solid background in human psychology and the interpersonal dynamics. Her reliable expertise is sought by television networks, reporters, political leaders, universities, professional associations, and bank and investor clients to translate complex subjects into easily understood and resolvable solutions. Ms. Olefson has lectured extensively and published multiple books and articles to educate the public as well as lawyers, realtors, bankers, investors, and mortgage brokers. As an engaging educator, Ms. Olefson plays a central role in the in-house training programs for some of the nation's leading lenders, investors and broker, corporations and organizations, translating complex subjects into easily understood and resolvable solutions. She is frequently quoted in such publications as the Wall Street Journal, Forbes, USA Today, Miami Herald, and MSNBC.com. She is interviewed on radio stations around the country and appears, often weekly, on CNBC, Fox News, MSNBC, PBS News Hour, NBC, CBS Evening News, CSPAN, and CNN as well as local television.

Ms. Olefson received her LLM from University of Miami, her JD from Benjamin N. Cardozo School of Law, and her BA from Carnegie Mellon University.

Acknowledgment: I would like to thank Audrey Anderson (legal assistant), Cheryl Hanby (paralegal), and David Blattner (shareholder), all of Fowler White Boggs PA, for their assistance with this chapter.

Understanding the Complexities of the Real Estate Transaction Process

Joel D. Rubin
*Partner and Co-Chair,
Institutional Real Estate Group*
Seyfarth Shaw LLP

ASPATORE

Introduction

I have attempted in this chapter to provide an understanding of transactional commercial real estate contracts and a framework for addressing complex real estate transactions, using a simple contract as the prototype, and discussing how to transition to the next level. Complex real estate transactions can take all different forms, and as a practitioner, you need to boil it all down to the basics, determine what the client seeks to achieve, and then reconstruct the transaction based on your and your teammates' prior experiences. Every time you are involved in a transaction, you need to pay attention to all aspects and store them in your mind. At some occasion in the future, something you did or heard before will become useful to what you are now being called upon to do.

Current Trends in Transactions

The interest in transactions for leased assets, especially on the coasts, is strong. Institutions and real estate funds with money have a desire to invest, and the debt market is very favorable (but could change at any time). In addition, certain retail projects that are only 80 percent occupied but with stable tenants in good locations are desirable, especially if the view is that the economy is recovering, albeit, slowly. In the case of institutions, joint ventures with operators for such retail assets are popular. Industrial properties are also in demand, again, depending on location, as leasing is picking up, although rents to date are well below three years ago. Needless to say, leased apartment projects are in high demand, especially in major metropolitan areas. The office sector, except for Class A fully leased properties, remains slow. The most difficult investments are 50 percent or more vacant projects that are leveraged. The owners of these projects are unwilling to spend money for tenant improvements and leasing commissions when the project is or could be under water, especially where the loan is coming due and new financing may not be available. Complicating matters further are the lenders/servicers whom are unwilling to write down the loan to the existing owner, and instead, drag their feet in taking control of the property.

The circumstances driving these trends, except in the case of apartments, are that the rates of return on the real estate investments are significantly higher than alternative investments and at reduced prices as compared to 2005 to 2007 (partially as a result of reduced rents), investors see opportunity. Real estate has always been considered a hedge against inflation, and many institutional investors see inflation as a risk that needs to be hedged. In the case of apartments, investors see substantial rent adjustments coming, especially in city locations as people have given up their homes to become renters. Further, with gas prices on the rise, people want to live closer to work and public transportation. With a limited supply of competitive product and short-term leases, apartment rents can be adjusted, quickly.

Common Structures

Today, limited liability companies are the most popular structure for commercial real estate transactions, unless the owner is a real estate investment trust (REIT). The limited liability company (LLC) offers favorable tax treatment, and the law governing LLCs has become well established in states such as Delaware. Other vehicles can be used to accomplish the goals of particular clients, and in some cases, a vehicle is chosen based on state and local tax issues. Lastly, the choice of vehicle may be controlled in part by the other parties to the transaction, including the lender. The fundamental issues in choosing a vehicle include federal, state, and local tax issues, including transfer taxes, and the needs of the investor—duties of loyalty and fair dealing, issues related to different types of tax-exempt investors such as pension funds or endowment funds, and the requirements of lenders.

Effective Practices for Commercial Real Estate Transactions

The Role of the Attorney

Lawyers who are at the top of their game need to take control of the transaction but in doing so must understand the needs and goals of their client. In a competitive environment, the ability to offer alternatives that satisfy the needs of all parties is important. While this may have been the case for many years, the pressure has increased because of the limited pool of good assets available and the highly competitive market. For those who are disposing of assets, there are issues of limiting continuing liability as well as creating structures that will qualify for 1031 tax treatment. The key to success is to know your client and to be well versed in alternative structures and approaches. Understand your client's goals and use your experiences to achieve them. If this is a new type of transaction, the Internet as well as fellow colleagues are a good initial source, but in the end, the burden falls on the practitioner to dissect the transaction into its various parts and solve each separately in order to get to the whole.

The Letter of Intent

Commercial real estate transactions for the most part start with a letter of intent (LOI) which may or may not be signed. The buyer usually initiates the LOI. If you represent the buyer, you may be consulted before the LOI is submitted to the seller. The most important part of the LOI is to make sure it is non-binding. The second most important part is to create some type of exclusive relationship while the contract is being negotiated. Lastly, the LOI should attempt to outline the structure of the transaction—if it is not an outright purchase/sale—and the allocation of costs—if such allocation is not going to follow local custom. The LOI can be a road map for the contract, but you want to avoid extensive negotiations at this stage and have the seller committed to the buyer for a short period to allow the parties to enter a contract.

Obviously, it is important to convince your client that you can add value by reviewing and discussing the LOI, but some clients move ahead without lawyers, especially where the environment is competitive, on the theory that all matters are subject to negotiation at the time of the contract. This may be true for noneconomic issues; however, to the extent there are tax implications to the way a transaction is structured, legal input at an early stage is important.

Meeting with the Client

Assuming you are past the LOI stage, it is important to sit with the client and understand the property, the client's goals, and the timing. Through the use of the Internet, you can develop a good understanding of the property and should be prepared to have a meaningful discussion with the client on property issues, tenant issues and vacancy, pending leasing, physical issues, and other items that could affect the transaction, such as the use of a tax free exchange under Section 1031 of the Internal Revenue Code (IRC). You should inquire about the existing financing on the property and what the intentions are regarding this from both a buyer's and seller's perspective. Most important to remember today is that time is your worst enemy; you need to move expeditiously, but at the client's speed, to bring the property under contract and consummate the transaction. In addition, it may be helpful to map the transaction process with the client. This will help all the parties on the team understand their respective roles, what steps are needed to accomplish the expected results and how, by understanding the process and creating a team with the client, costs can be controlled.

Following the Contract

The real estate contract controls the transaction. All the terms of the deal must be contained in the contract. Today, it is customary that all the closing documents are exhibits to the contract. In most cases, the contract provides for a due diligence period on the part of the buyer before the buyer is committed to complete the purchase, although a good faith deposit in escrow is usually made, either concurrently with or within a short period after signing. Sometimes the deposit is increased when the buyer waives due diligence. In some states, a token consideration payment is made at contract signing to support the existence of a binding contract, even though the buyer can terminate for any reason. In New York City, sellers have been able, in many cases, to require that due diligence be completed before contract signing, which puts the buyer at risk of a topping offer after the buyer has spent significant dollars on legal fees and due diligence costs.

If you are the seller, it is important that all due diligence materials be assembled well in advance of a possible sale and reviewed by the appropriate parties to avoid surprises. Appendix H includes a checklist to be used in preparation for a sale. Again, time is your enemy, so delays in deliveries or surprises set back transactions. Lastly, not all due diligence items in the seller's possession such as proprietary materials, physical reports, and similar items need to be delivered to a prospective buyer. However, some sellers are willing to deliver recent environmental reports to avoid any future claims regarding the same. In any case, the contract should be specific as to what is excluded.

The typical contract includes:

- A description of what is being purchased
- The earnest money deposit
- The excluded due diligence materials
- The contingency period
- Title and survey matters, including the types of exceptions seller is required to cure and the form of title policy that needs to be issued as a condition of closing
- Representations and warranties of seller—which in many case are more limited in scope than a few years ago
- Tied to the representations and warranties are remedies for their breaches: what are the rights of buyer for a pre-closing breach, what is the effect of buyer's knowledge on post-closing claims, and the survival period for making claims
- Rights and obligations of seller during the period before close of due diligence and between the end of due diligence and closing—e.g. maintenance, capital repairs, leasing, and the costs associated with each
- Changes in property condition—e.g., new building code violations and changes in tenancy such as tenant bankruptcies after the close of due diligence
- The closing process
- Tenant estoppel requirements
- Prorations—beware of issues such as real estate taxes which may be affected by state and local law
- Tenant reimbursements and responsibility for billing tenants post-closing for pre-closing reimbursements
- Casualty and condemnation
- Releases of seller and "as is" provisions
- Assignment rights on the part of seller and buyer, including anti-flip provisions
- Local law contract requirements
- Deal specific matters such as holdbacks and escrows

It is customary today to have monetary limitations on seller's liabilities for breaches of its representations and warranties that are first discovered post-closing. Some contracts include arbitration provisions, but such dispute resolution provisions may encourage disputes. In the case of institutions and major players, there is an underlying philosophy that the parties will see each other again, and unless there is an egregious issue, most issues are resolved by the business people on both sides.

Understanding the Contract

To effectively represent a client it is important that you understand every aspect of the real estate contract and how provisions relate to each other. Thus, you are better able to negotiate changes and reach meaningful compromises. For instance, the time period between end of due diligence and closing may affect your position on leasing during this period or on the risk of a casualty. And how are you handling loss of rents from a pre-closing casualty, since buyer's insurance does not cover this because the triggering event occurred pre-closing. Again, contracts can be complex depending on the issues, and the best advice is to understand the issues completely. Once you understand the underlying concerns, you can be better prepared to address the issues. For instance, what is the difference between an assumption of an obligation and an indemnity? Is indemnity needed, if buyer assumes the obligation? Is there concern about contractual liability, tort liability or legal liability to the federal, state, or local governmental entity?

Do Not Forget the Tax Issues

Part and parcel of all transactions is the tax treatment. Some institutional owners are tax exempt, and different tax exempt entities have different issues such as on the treatment of debt financed income. Certain tax exempts may in certain cases qualify for exemption under local transfer tax provisions. One partner of a partnership cannot complete a 1031 trade since the partner owns a partnership interest and not real estate. Most owners and buyers use pass-through entities such as limited liability companies, but state and local tax considerations may affect the choice of the ownership entity. In some cases, private REITs are used to avoid local tax issues, and in many cases, REITs will use Qualified REIT Subsidiaries instead of single member limited liability companies to minimize local taxes. The preferred vehicle today for joint ventures is a limited liability company since a limited partnership requires a general partner, which in most cases must have some investment in the transaction, but joint ventures have their own tax issues, especially where one of the members is tax exempt.

The Challenges

It is a pleasure to work with good lawyers on the other side of a transaction, especially those who are motivated to reach the same overall objective of consummating a transaction. Treat this as a learning experience: do not try to show that you are smarter than your opposing counsel. Work as a team. In significant transactions with significant players, no one is looking to take advantage of the other, and in some cases trying to do so can backfire. As suggested above, the same players are likely to be back at the table on another deal in the future, and poor behavior here can poison the well. Further, the group of players in the sophisticated area of large complex transactions is small, and word travels fast. In a competitive environment, overreaching on one deal could easily keep your client off the list of finalists in the next transaction, even where the parties are different. Think of you and your opposing counsel as problem solvers, working together to achieve what the clients expected when they shook hands on the deal.

The challenge is when opposing counsel is not on the same page, seeks to overreach or attempts to masquerade his ignorance and the going gets rough. The best advice in such situations is to keep it simple and at the same time ask your client to have separate discussions with his counterpart. Avoid, however, in these cases, joint meetings or calls with both attorneys and clients, since embarrassing the other lawyer in front of his client is never a path to success. Lastly, as suggested above, boil the issues down to the lowest level: think them through so that you can explain them on the simplest of levels. To accomplish this is a true measure of how good a lawyer you are. By doing so, you will at least keep your own client on your side, or if your client thinks the issue not to be important, he may advise you to compromise it or let it go. Remember, no matter how complex the matter, your client views this as a process, and you will be judged, not on your brilliance, but on how well you managed the process. Do not underestimate your client: not only does he pay your bills but he is also part of the team. Yes, your responsibility is to protect the client, but you need to understand the risks and explain them to the client. He is the person who has evaluated the transaction, and if you explain the issues in a manner he can understand, he can and will provide you with valuable input and make the decision whether to assume the risk. Remember it is his transaction, not yours. You are merely a facilitator, albeit a smart one and even smarter if you understand your role.

Conclusion

Participating in transactional real estate can be rewarding and exciting. The issues run from the mundane to the complex. It provides a great opportunity to experience and learn how clients approach issues and reach resolutions. I have seen mundane economic issues such as how to split closing costs settled by throwing quarters against the wall. And I have seen noneconomic matters debated for hours, in some cases, based on poor lawyering, or in other cases, based on undisclosed and somewhat unrelated issues, which becomes very frustrating. But remember what your role is and try to learn from every experience.

The more you know and understand the better you will be able to address issues. And most importantly, listen to what the others are saying and adapt accordingly. Lawyers tend to think they know it all and fail to listen.

The market has come back, but because the number of investment grade properties on the market are much fewer, the market is highly competitive, and thus, in many cases the transactions are complex. These are challenging times, made even more so by the time demands of the clients and their transaction counterparts. Adapt and enjoy.

Key Takeaways

- Strive for excellence.
- Know your client and be well versed in alternative structures and approaches.
- Store whatever you learn on a matter since it may well become useful in the future.

- Break the issue down to the smallest common denominator: can you explain it to a novice and achieve understanding?
- Move expeditiously—but at the client's speed—to bring the property under contract and consummate the transaction.
- In reality, you as the lawyer are managing a process and will be judged on how well you accomplished your client's (not your) goals.
- Listen before you respond. It is amazing how much more you will learn which will make you more effective.
- Never compromise your principles and ethics: clients come and go but most important is your reputation as an excellent lawyer.

Joel D. Rubin is a partner at Seyfarth Shaw LLP and co-chair of the firm's Institutional Real Estate Group. With more than thirty-five years of experience in pension fund, real estate, and corporate law, Mr. Rubin provides strategic planning and legal advice to public and private pension funds, their investment advisors, foreign investors, REITs and developers regarding real estate investments throughout the United States. He has extensive experience in organizing and planning co-investments, joint ventures, and REITs; acquiring and disposing of income-producing properties; and financing developments and re-developments. Mr. Rubin, also, has significant experience in advising clients regarding the fiduciary responsibilities of funds and their advisors and acts as legal counselor to businesses in a variety of areas, including riverboat and Indian gaming. He is a businessperson's lawyer, acting as the point person in advising and managing the business/legal process, including litigation, for clients. Mr. Rubin has an AV rating in Martindale Hubbell, and is listed in Chambers USA *as a leading lawyer for real estate in Illinois.*

Practical Aspects of Commercial Real Estate Transactions

Alfred M. Meyerson
Partner
Thompson & Knight LLP

ASPATORE

Introduction

I have been practicing law for twenty-six years, and my current practice is split primarily between representing real estate developers or borrowers on the one hand, and representing lenders on the other. This work includes all forms of commercial real estate: office buildings, multifamily apartment projects, retail shopping centers, and industrial buildings. In addition, I also work on the occasional hotel, golf course, and condominium regime.

My experience sets me apart from most lawyers insofar as I regularly represent both sides of real estate transactions. Through representing both borrowers and lenders, I have learned what each party wants versus what it needs, which gives me a better sense of which aspects of the transactions are negotiable and which aren't.

Also, my years of experience have given me a sense of practicality—not all legal issues are equally important, nor are they always treated the same. As economic and other circumstances change, the practical approach to solving problems must evolve as well.

Trends in the Real Estate Practice Area

Finding Distressed Assets

During the last year, I have seen the national focus of our clients directed toward opportunities in "distressed real estate assets." These assets could be real property or debt secured by real property, either of which can be troubled since the recent downturn in the economy. Clients are looking for good deals in the real estate market and are hoping to find either desperate property owners who need to liquidate their assets or desperate banks pressured by regulators to address under-secured or otherwise non-performing loans. When the market dropped, investors envisioned a "crash and burn" real estate debacle, similar to what occurred in the 1980s. But, in reality, it has been a much softer landing. Several equity funds have been set up to take advantage of the expected down market, but in reality, most of these funds have not been able to find nearly as much "product" as expected. So, while there have been some foreclosures and sales of debt, they have not occurred in the anticipated volume.

Multifamily Development

On the positive side, in Texas, we are seeing quite a bit of new activity with multifamily apartment projects, which have become the hot product for 2011. As anecdotal evidence, we are currently representing a few different banks that are making several construction loans for new apartment projects. In addition, there are a number of instances in which we are representing multifamily developers that have equity investors competing to invest in their project while four or more banks are bidding to provide the construction financing for the same project. These projects are all in the Houston area and slated to commence development during 2011.

There are several reasons that multifamily projects are currently so popular—the simplest of which is that many people are unable to afford to buy a house or are concerned about the long-term nature of a thirty-year mortgage while there may be some uncertainty about their jobs. There is also an entire generation of young adults graduating from college, coming into the workforce, who just aren't interested in buying a house. They are more mobile and prefer a more "upscale" lifestyle, which is affordable with monthly rent. The new apartments are being built in areas with growing populations, and Texas has the good fortune to be one of the few strong growth areas relative to the rest of the country.

The result is all sorts of investors and lenders are anxious to be in the Texas multifamily market, especially since the bond market is currently providing a miserable rate of return and the stock market is not considered by some to be as stable an investment as Class A apartments. Therefore, investors are happy to receive 5 to 6 percent on their money with potential long-term upside. And, while these returns are historically low, there are very few other options for most investors.

The Growth of Industrial Real Estate

Finally, industrial properties are particularly popular in the Houston area, especially those near the Port of Houston that provide manufacturing or warehousing for businesses related to the oil and gas business. Whether its pipes, drill bits, or other tools of the trade, given the current high demand for oil and gas based products, these industrial based commercial properties are expected to maintain their value.

The Impact of Trends on the Practice Area

Lawyers in the real estate practice area are getting busier as lenders and borrowers continue to grow their businesses. And, as we are beginning to do more deals, our processes have evolved based on "lessons learned" from this recent real estate downturn. For example, from a lender's perspective, as underwriting standards have become more stringent, we have tightened up loan guaranties. Also, as the use of receiverships has become more common, we have redrafted the relevant loan document provisions to more clearly set forth parameters for receiverships.

Facilitating a Successful Commercial Real Estate Transaction

In commercial real estate deals, we are generally dealing with very sophisticated parties, such as developers, equity investors, and institutional lenders. Equity investors are generally life insurance companies, pension funds, university endowments, or private funds that have been created for these types of investments. Their equity is invested with the developer, who will then leverage that investment with third party debt. There are limited opportunities for developers in this economy, so if a developer finds the perfect piece of property for a commercial project, equity investors desperately want to be a partner in the deal and the banks will be vying to provide the debt.

Once a project has been conceived and the right real estate found, developers then present the opportunity to prospective partners (i.e., the equity investors) or lenders (e.g., commercial banks). If they are interested, we lay out the basics of the deal (e.g., purchase price for the land, length of time to close, sharing of closing costs, etc.) via a letter of intent. Ideally, our clients involve us at this stage of the process, because we can provide valuable counsel on how best to structure these terms. Once the letter of intent is agreed upon, we prepare a comprehensive purchase and sale agreement to buy the land, which contains all of the terms of the sale—from general to the smallest detail.

At the same time, we will work with the developer as he negotiates the terms with his equity partners. Those terms of the partnership can vary widely. In some instances, the equity partners provide all of the capital necessary for a project and, in some, they invest "side by side" with the developer who invests alongside the equity partner. Accordingly, as the investment risk spectrum shifts, so too does the expected rate of return for the equity partner. A typical scenario would provide the equity partner with a "preferred return" of 8 to 12 percent, followed by a return of all capital, before the developer would be entitled to its portion of the capital distribution (which, again, is negotiable). Of course, the developer is earning income along the way in the manner of development fees, construction management fees, property management fees, and the like. As stated earlier, we prefer to begin negotiations with a letter of intent to help the partners set expectations and agree upon the business terms before we spend the time (and client's money) drafting a partnership agreement.

Finally, when dealing with lenders, the parties use a term sheet to serve the same purpose as the letter of intent; that is, to confirm agreement on the basic terms of the loan (e.g., loan amount, interest rate, maturity, etc.) Once these have all been agreed upon, the lender's lawyers draft loan documents, and the documentation negotiation process begins. Again, experience has taught that we can provide the most value to our clients when we get involved early in this process.

Utilizing a Thorough Checklist

The single most important document in a real estate transaction is also the simplest one—the master checklist. There are simply too many different things going on simultaneously for anyone to be sure that all tasks are being done and being done in a timely manner. This checklist contains the names of the parties involved—the lender, lawyers, equity partners, contact people, title company, and the various parties to the transaction. We include all of their contact information and we go through each segment of the deal to cover the different documents for each segment. There is also the real estate due diligence portion for such items as title and survey, entitlements, utilities, and environmental assessment. We keep track of the legal documents that need to be prepared for the formation of the development entity, the property conveyance, and the third party financing.

Client Strategies

The Initial Client Meeting

When clients seek our help, they generally already have a deal in process and believe they already know what they want. In an effort to reduce their legal costs, they often put off seeing a lawyer until they have something definitive. When they do come to us, we try to discern their ultimate goal because it can differ significantly from client to client and from deal to deal. For example, some developers want to buy land, build a project, and sell it immediately. Others want to buy, build, and hold onto it forever. Different clients have different intentions, and the best real estate attorneys are able to elicit each client's motivations and goals. With this understanding, the attorney can tailor his counsel for each transaction accordingly, because the advice may change depending on the client's circumstances. We walk with the client through each phase of the transaction to assure that we are still focused on achieving the client's short-term and long-term goals.

Setting Client Expectations and Answering Questions

Most importantly, real estate attorneys must understand and help set expectations for the client because every client is different. Some clients want to suffer through every detail with their attorneys and are disappointed if they don't get the opportunity to evaluate every paragraph of every document, while others prefer the "30,000 foot" view and expect the attorneys to take care of the entire situation—yet most fall somewhere in between.

One of the keys to becoming an effective member of the client's real estate team is understanding the full context of each deal. Just as every client is different, every transaction is different based on its own circumstances and context.

When working with new clients, it is important for lawyers to be thorough when interviewing the client to learn their expectations. Clients who want to avoid all detail are quick to make it clear that they are not interested in "how to make a watch"—they just want to know what time it is. But lawyers should never judge too quickly, since I have had several clients who pretend they are not interested in the detail, until they start a lengthy inquiry into certain issues. Eventually, the dedicated lawyer will discern each client's expectations and work to achieve them.

Common Legal Mistakes

From the developer's perspective, the most common mistakes I have observed arose from either lawyers or their clients failing to conduct comprehensive due diligence. For example, some real estate developers completely skip the necessary environmental work before buying a property, or fail to have their acquisition funding fully in place before they commit to buy a property. The most detrimental mistakes have been those where aspects of due diligence were ignored either due to ignorance or some unwarranted optimism. The point is that most mistakes can be avoided with due care and good counsel.

On the bank's side of the equation, the biggest mistakes were made years ago—making loans on projects that (with the benefit of hindsight) never should have been made. Now that it has become very difficult for borrowers to repay their loans, banks are often faced with the decision of whether to foreclose on a property or grant concessions to the borrower in hopes that the borrower's business improves. If the bank does foreclose, then it will own the property and have to deal with the issues of ownership. If not, the bank can let the borrower continue to own and manage the property, which frequently makes sense, because in most cases the borrower is much more adept at doing so. Therefore, if the bank does not believe the borrower is stealing or misapplying rental income, it is not uncommon for the bank to allow the borrower to continue to own and manage the property in hopes that things will eventually improve. After all, just because a bank takes back a shopping center in foreclosure, it does not mean that it will suddenly fill with rent paying tenants. Most of the time, the toughest decision for the bank is the judgment call as to who is best suited to manage the distressed asset—the bank or the borrower.

Conclusion

The makeup of many of our clients has changed in recent years. In Texas, clients are coming from all over the world because our locale has become one of the top national targets for investors. In the past, New York City,

Washington, D.C., Boston, and the West Coast were at the top of every list of investment opportunities. The sovereign funds, in particular, were the most select and looked only at the premier buildings in the absolute strongest markets. But in today's market they are all now looking for opportunities in Texas, because of the strong energy economy, which has created a positive employment growth rate. Simply put, real estate development follows jobs.

Accordingly, more activity in commercial real estate has been predicted for the next year or two. In particular, the expectation is there will be more multifamily projects and targeted industrial growth, with a reduced interest in retail development. There will be limited office growth because we appear to have enough available space, unless there are single users who decide to build their own buildings in some sub-markets.

Successful Real Estate Attorneys

The best advice for real estate attorneys who are working on these types of transactions is to try to know the real estate market. While good lawyers know the legal issues, the best lawyers also know the current market. For example, time spent today on negotiating key issues of three years ago is time wasted. As the market changes, what's available to a client and what isn't evolves, and the best lawyers are those who have the best sense of what is current. Lawyers are not doing their clients any favors by making demands they will never get, or giving unnecessary concessions.

In addition to legal periodicals, the best real estate practitioners study industry literature as well. Continuing legal education conferences can be just as valuable as client industry conferences. While real estate lawyers are not expected to know as much as their clients do about the real estate business, a comprehensive understanding is invaluable to being the best real estate lawyer.

Key Takeaways

- Create a master checklist in every real estate transaction that includes all of the basic information for all parties involved. This will help keep the transaction organized from beginning to end.

- Explain to clients the importance of obtaining legal help early in the real estate transaction process to avoid mistakes and make the best, most cost-efficient plan for the deal.
- Always start with a letter of intent to make sure there is a meeting of the minds before launching into expensive and time-consuming legal documentation.
- Complete your due diligence throughout the entire real estate transaction process. Most mistakes occur because of ignoring due diligence and failing to take the time to thoroughly evaluate the deal, step by step.
- Know your industry. The best lawyers are experts in both the law and industry of their specialized area.

Alfred M. Meyerson, a partner with Thompson & Knight LLP and the leader of the Houston office, focuses his practice on all aspects of commercial real estate transactions, including leases (retail, office, industrial, and ground leases), purchase and sale agreements, development agreements, construction contracts, joint venture/partnership agreements, note purchase agreements, including extensive experience representing borrowers and lenders with interim, permanent, and construction financing, as well as debt restructuring, workouts, foreclosures, and the subsequent sale of REO and other distressed assets.

Mr. Meyerson has been selected for inclusion in the Chambers USA Leaders in Their Field and The Legal 500 US directories. The Legal 500 US states Mr. Meyerson is "an exceptional attorney who is dedicated and easy to work with." He is board certified in commercial real estate law by the Texas Board of Legal Specialization.

Clients consider Mr. Meyerson "an excellent and gifted real estate attorney who is both innovative and responsive and whose knowledge of all aspects of real estate law is unsurpassed" according to The Best Lawyers in America.

Mr. Meyerson received his JD from The University of Texas School of Law and his BA, with highest honors, from The University of Texas at Austin, Phi Beta Kappa.

Legal Issues Associated with Integrated Construction Contracting

Kevin J. Connolly
Shareholder
Anderson Kill & Olick PC

ASPATORE

Introduction

Anthropologists recognize that the "built environment" is one of the characteristics that distinguishes our culture from its caveman progenitors. *See, e.g.*, Amos Rapoport, "Spatial Organization and the Built Environment" in *Companion Encyclopedia of Anthropology* (Routledge, London 1994). We undertake few activities that are not affected by or make use of real estate, and much of this activity involves the creation, alteration, or use of buildings and other things that are constructed. For all that, it is fundamental to human society, construction remains a risk-laden activity. Construction requires attention to risk, and it is worthwhile to adopt a broad understanding of risks.

Ultimately, the foremost risk of construction is the risk of non-completion of the work. In order for an owner or developer to undertake the manifold risks of construction, there must be a perception that the completed construction has a value that exceeds the "palpable risk." In other words, no owner or developer undertakes construction unless it expects the benefits of the completed construction to outweigh the costs—fixed and contingent—that are anticipated.

Construction contracts are a way of transferring and sharing risks associated with the project. Before construction begins and before contracts are awarded, the risk of non-completion is completely on the owner: if he does nothing, he will reap nothing. By awarding a contract for construction, the owner is relieved of the legal risk of non-completion: so long as the owner performs his side of the contract (and assuming the contract is well drawn), if the contractor does not complete the project then the contractor is answerable in damages.

As always, the devil is in the details. "Integrated Construction Contracting" is an approach to contract award that recognizes that the entire construction contract (not just the construction drawings) should be coordinated in order to optimize the contract as a tool for allocating risks in advance of losses. "Allocate now or litigate later."[1]

---

[1] I ascribe this aphorism to Stanley Sklar, who used it as a subtitle for a continuing legal education course that he moderated through the Practising Law Institute.

Integrated Construction Contracting: Practical and Legal Considerations

In construction, it is often said that problems are created where one trade leaves off and another trade begins its work. As a matter of contract, it is the general contractor who takes responsibility for making the different components of the construction process fit together, but as a practical matter it is sometimes necessary to force the two trades to coordinate their activity to produce finished, continuous construction.

Plans and specifications also need to be coordinated. For complex projects, these design documents are prepared by many different professionals: structural engineers for roofs, walls, and framing; mechanical engineers for heating, ventilating, air conditioning and elevators; plumbing engineers for water, sanitation, and fire protection; electrical engineers for power and computer cabling; and sometimes more. In its simplest form, "coordination" means ensuring that these different designers do not all end up trying to use the same 4'x4' riser to serve the entire building. Common practice today recognizes that some part of the design process has to include coordination of the designs, and good contracting practice includes a variety of tools for identifying the points where coordination is necessary and allocating responsibility for carrying it out.

Coordination of the Construction Contract

For many construction projects, that is as far as coordination goes. Typically, the lawyers tell the architect to ensure that the consultants' design documents are coordinated with each other, and the architect must coordinate his design with the design of the consultants. For other projects, coordination takes a further step, as the construction manager reviews the design during development and makes comments on feasibility and economy.

There remains a significant area where coordination is almost totally lacking, and that is the construction contract itself. A simple model for construction contracting—one that has been adopted by all of the major industry bodies, including the American Institute of Architects, Associated General Contractors, and Engineers Joint Contract Documents

Committee—is to make reference to the final design documents and document the contractor's promise to build the described work within a stated time for a fixed price. Of course, no lawyer could possibly leave it at that: there must be terms and conditions that govern the rights and responsibilities of the parties before, during, and after the performance of the work.

It seems that most lawyers have a standard repertoire of contract terms that they apply to construction contracts on a one size fits all basis. In this vein, it is common for the lawyers' documents to provide that the documents that they prepare—contract, general, and supplementary conditions—displace all other contract documents. One of the problems with this approach lies in the fact that the lawyers are not running the project. The lead professional on a construction project is typically an architect, who has his own preferred terms and conditions. He will embody those terms in the general requirements of the project, and there is no reason to expect that he will subordinate his favored documents to the lawyer's documents.

A far better approach is for the lawyer to actually review the project manual—the bound volume that contains the general requirements, specifications and other terms. The project manual typically contains terms relevant to payment applications, change orders, claims, liens, warranties, and the closeout of the construction project. Instead of simply stepping all over the architect's documents, the lawyer should approach the architect's work with the respect that is due to a learned professional. When the architect's terms are wrong—such as expressing a waiver of lien rights before construction commences—the lawyer should correct the error. However, in judgment matters, the lawyer should not assume that his judgment is correct. Even if the lawyer is correct, he should be mindful that the lawyer cannot vet every decision and action of the architect.

Instead of making the lawyer's documents control the legal obligations of the parties, it is better to adopt a more conciliatory approach. The American Institute of Architects forms provide that all of the forms that make up the contract are to be read together and harmonized to the extent possible. The one lawyerly adjustment that should be endorsed in this setting is the provision that if it is impossible to harmonize the terms of the documents, then they should be construed to require the greater quantity, higher quality, and sooner completion of the relevant work.

By taking an approach that recognizes that the lawyer is just one member of the team, counsel can not only produce a better contract, but he can also begin the process of team building that often proves critical in achieving a successful project. If the team has been abused by counsel and treated with disrespect, the lawyer may receive a reminder that what goes around comes around. If the lawyer conducts himself professionally and keeps an open mind during contract award and afterward, he will find that the participants can come together and put the completion of the project first on their respective priority lists.

Contract Formats and Components

The industry bodies publish more or less elaborate forms of contract terms that are coordinated with the one or more basic contract forms that they publish. Many lawyers eschew the use of industry standard forms, and others amend the standard form into an unrecognizable mass of nonsense, but all of these contract models have this in common: they document a contractual obligation on the contractor to build the work and on the owner to pay for it.

Recognizing Nonsense

To a certain extent, recognizing that a provision has gone beyond the pale calls for the experience. However, adopting a risk-aware approach to negotiations is frequently helpful. For example, we sometimes see contracts that prescribe that the contractor will perform all of the "work" required by (including that implied in) the contract documents, and which then lists those contract documents to include drawings, specifications, the signed contract and its riders, change orders, bulletins, and amendments

That list is entirely ordinary except for its inclusion of bulletins. A bulletin normally does not become a contract document until it is accepted by the contractor as part of a change order. By including bulletins in the contract documents, the owner might be said to be trying to capture the right to

51

impose unilateral changes in the contract. Now the contractor who wants to resist those unilateral changes can resort to several compelling arguments.

First and foremost of these antidotes are the limitations that the law imposes on "Incorporation by Reference." Two parties entering into a contract may stipulate that the contract that they are signing should be construed by reading it together with some other document, which is "deemed" to be part of the contract being signed. This is paradigmatic of construction contracts, which incorporate many parts: owner-contractor agreement, general conditions of the contract, supplementary conditions of the contract, specifications, drawings, amendments, and addenda. The best practice for incorporation by reference is to attach the referenced documents to the document being signed, so that there is no doubt as to identity and content of the incorporated document.

However, sometimes we see "master" forms of contract—most often subcontracts—that reference documents that have not come into existence at the time that the master form is adopted. This could be overcome by entering into letter agreements on a project-by-project basis and using those letter agreements as the point of incorporation by reference of the master documents and the documents for the current project. This is not an exaltation of form over substance. It is a recognition that most construction contracts are formed without the advice of lawyers. The opportunities for overreaching are abundant, and the opportunities are exploited to a degree that is sometimes scandalous.[2] We still see contracts tendered for execution on a "no comments—take it or leave it" basis that nonetheless provide that the contractor surrenders the right to file a mechanic's lien. Most states' laws provide that a waiver embedded in the construction contract is absolutely void, though a few states' laws explicitly validate such a waiver. A demand for such a waiver in, e.g., New York, is a red flag that your counterpart has a bad attitude. How you cope with such bad attitudes is a matter for the art and science of negotiation. But be aware that there are parties whose counsel insists on such nonsense.

---

[2] Much of the restraints on these behaviors are found in the trust fund provisions of some states' construction codes. New York's Lien Law is especially draconic for the readiness with which an unwitting owner can become guilty of larceny under McKinney's New York Lien Law §79. The intricacies of these codes are beyond the scope of this chapter, whose focus is the contract award process, since this represents the point at which counsel's impact is most profound and persistent.

One of the recurrent sources of problems consists of areas of joint interest and concern. Lawyers will want to pay attention to payment terms. The architect has an interest here as well, especially if he is expected to sign off on the contractor's invoices. The architect may have included terms governing payment in the specifications for the project. This is not an unwarranted extension of the architect's responsibility: it is part of his standard of care. Money is the lifeblood of construction, and an architect who fails to attend to that grim reality is one who fails his client.

General Requirements

There are many, many terms that can be found in the "general requirements" division of the specification that overlap with the "general and supplementary conditions of the contract" that lawyers like to promulgate. The overlap can get worse: many architects will include their very own version of general and supplementary conditions in the bid package that is previewed by contractors. If a judge or arbitrator cannot reconcile or harmonize the conflicting parts of the overlapping documents, he may decide that they are repugnant and cancel each other out. This can happen even if the lawyer's document says that his documents trump all other documents in the event of a conflict.

When a court or arbitrator finds that contract terms cancel each other out, there is a hole in the contract at a point where more than one person believed contract terms were needed. Sometimes, the process that results is in the nature of *cy pres* proceedings in which a tribunal tries to divine what the parties would have agreed to had they recognized the problem. At other times, the absence of a contract term means that a gap-filling statute will step up and complete the contract for the parties. Perhaps not on the terms that the parties would have settled upon, but the terms of the statute are the default agreement that the legislature has written for us. A good example is the New York Construction Contracts Act, Article 35-E of McKinney's New York General Business Law, which prescribes a schedule for payments and an exclusive list of grounds for dishonoring an invoice for construction services, but which provides that the parties can elect out of most of the terms of the statute.

One of the time-honored methods of controlling the contract is the project manual. This is a book (or several volumes) that is intended to be considered together with the drawings when seeking to bid on or negotiate for a project. Good project manuals include the form of contract, including general and supplementary conditions so that when a contractor tenders a bid or proposal, he is expected to accept the terms and conditions as laid down by the owner. In some cases, the owner conducts a pre-bid conference at which interested parties express "comments" on the requirements of the bid package. To the extent that the owner elects to change the terms of the solicitation, the new terms are generally written up as an "addendum" instead of reissuing the project manual. A contractor who does not even raise a concern about terms in the project manual will generally not be heard to complain only when a dispute has arisen.

Clarification by Judges and Arbiters

One of the reasons why judges and arbitrators sometimes disregard some or all of the "armor plating" that lawyers dream up is eminently practical: construction contracts are complex with lots of moving parts. The best way to understand something this complex is to see how it operates in practice. This is known as "practical construction," and its wisdom lies in looking at how the parties behave themselves in order to figure out what their agreements actually call for. In practice, the lawyer is not involved in the project day by day, week by week, or even month by month. The project is run by the contractor, with the architect looking over his shoulder from time to time. In this setting, the lawyer should anticipate that his fine legal drafting will come to naught and the project will be run in the way that the architect anticipated.

Experienced lawyers know that their documents should "speak to the transaction"—the documents must reflect the reality of the parties' deal. This requires the lawyer to dig into the project manual a little deeper than usual. It is not enough simply to incorporate the specifications by reference: someone has to look at the other parts of the contract, especially the general requirements, and coordinate the legal terms and conditions with the practices and procedures laid down by the design professionals. Failure to carry out this step might undermine confidence that there has actually been a meeting of the minds. The result can be claims far in excess of the expected contract sum.

Lawyers who do not bring prior experience or relevant education to the practice of construction law will find themselves daunted by the overwhelming amounts of information available in print and electronic form. One of the most useful places to begin is the Architect's Manual of Professional Practice. This four-volume loose-leaf service is invaluable for its organization, clarity, and comprehensiveness. Also useful are the documents published by the AIA, AGC, and/or EJCDC in electronic format with substantial accompanying educational materials.

Among these are two especially useful documents: A-521, Uniform Location of Subject Matter, and B-163, Owner-Architect Agreement for Designated Services. Neither of these is included in the current AIA forms library, but they are included in the Architect's Manual noted above. A-521 was originally intended to harmonize the different terminology employed by architects and engineers when referring to the same entities. The uses of the A-521 are greater, however, because it directs contract-drafters to incorporate related terms in a predictable location. Studying the A-521 gives the lawyer insight into the wide variety of documents that can be incorporated into a construction contract and the distinct roles that they play. Since all contract documents are required to be read together, any given term—whether it be an anti-lien provision, a limitation on extra charges, terms governing claims, or any of hundreds of different provisions—could be located in any contract document. However, certain terms *belong* in the owner-constructor agreement (e.g., timing, price, and reference to the catalog of documents that are part of this contract) while others belong in the contract conditions (e.g., responsibility of contractor for subcontractors' acts and omissions, required insurance, limitations on claims) while others belong in the specifications. Understanding where a contract provision belongs not only makes the document more coherent, it also illuminates the division of responsibility of the parties. The agreement and conditions are preeminently the responsibility of counsel, while specifications are the bailiwick of architects and engineers.

The B-163 form includes a comprehensive table of activities relating to the whole development cycle. From site selection and qualification (including marketing feasibility studies as well as zoning due diligence and subsurface investigations) through project conceptualization, construction, commissioning, turnover, and post-occupancy issues, the B-163 tabulates a wide variety of activities that are critical to successful projects. In addition, the B-163 illustrates a model of contract drafting that encourages clarity, simplicity, and flexibility that is useful in non-construction settings as well.

Finally, there are citatory services published by the AIA that report on court decisions (as well as those rare arbitral awards that enter the public domain, usually through court review) and correlate those decisions with the multitudinous forms that are published. A final area for lawyers to hone their skills is in the subject of insurance. Insurance litigation arising out of construction is pestilential in its incidence and in the impossibility of curbing the continuing flow of disputes.

Ultimately, players in construction can improve their bottom line by reducing the amount of disputes that require formal resolution. One way to control the disputes and their cost is to recognize the risks before losses occur, and to allocate them by contract.

Contracts as a Cost-Control Mechanism

Part of the purpose behind entering into a written construction contract is cost control. In cases of imperfect coordination of contract documents, there is always a risk that some parts of the work will fall "out of scope." That is simply construction terminology for an increase in the price payable by the owner. These glitches represent failures of the contract documents to achieve the cost control that the owner desired. I have sometimes been criticized for undertaking reviews of specifications because it is beyond the duty of care owed by lawyers to their clients. I am not sanguine about that conclusion: to the extent that an uncoordinated contract produces a loss for one's client, there is an avoidable bad outcome, and I do not believe that the law would assign 100 percent of the responsibility for this to the architect or to the owner. The lawyer is the one who deals in contracts, and the lawyer is certainly at risk, if only a litigation risk.

Among the special challenges of construction dispute resolution is the hard fact that delaying the project while disputes are resolved can spell doom for the project. The AIA contract forms epitomize a "build now—fight later" approach. Central to the AIA contract model is the use of a third party to provide an initial determination. That third party has in the past usually been the architect, though current practice allows for a neutral who has no stake in the project. Regardless of how the umpire is selected, the concept is to enable a prompt but preliminary determination of the parties' rights. Thus, a contractor may claim that it is entitled to extra compensation because it claims that work demanded by the owner is actually "out of scope," or because the owner has failed to make the site available for the contractor to operate. The umpire makes an initial decision—e.g., that the contractor's claim is only partially correct and the owner owes some extra compensation for the work (but not as much as the contractor is seeking). If the owner does not pay the amount directed by the umpire, then the owner is in breach of contract and the contractor can stop work and file liens and lawsuits. If the contractor refuses to perform the work unless it receives the full payment that it seeks, then the contractor is in breach and can be replaced. These interim solutions apply even if at the time the smoke clears it turns out that the contractor's claim should have been allowed for the full amount, or if the owner should not have had to pay anything because all of the demanded work was included in the base contract work.

In other words, a construction contract needs to have a continued-work-pending-dispute clause, because a project would be doomed if every difference of opinion entitled the owner to stop paying or contractor to stop working. Likewise, when mechanics' liens are filed, the contractor may insist that it is the owner's fault for not paying the extras that were demanded. But the contract will usually require the contractor to file a bond to discharge the liens and defer the fight over payment until the court or arbitration hearings are concluded.

Insurance and Risk Management in Construction Projects

There remains an important join between the documents discussed thus far—plans, specifications, contract and contract conditions—and the work product of yet another kind of professional: the risk manager. In the context of writing construction contracts, "risk management" is simply a twenty-five-cent word for "insurance."

Insurance is important to construction. A person in the construction business who is not properly insured is sitting on a time bomb: sooner or later, he will be out of business, likely with a bang. All of the participants have interests in insurance and, one would think, an interest in making sure that all the appropriate insurance has been purchased. Nonetheless, inept insurance clauses are distressingly common. We still see mandates for "comprehensive public liability insurance with the broad form comprehensive property damage rider," coverage for "fire & lightning with extended coverage, vandalism and malicious mischief," and like references to insurance forms that have been obsolete and unavailable for more than twenty-five years.

Today, the construction contract is sure to include insurance terms. The lawyer may beef up the insurance terms by amplifying the kinds of insurance required, and typically dictates additional legends that must appear on the certificates of insurance. Regardless of whether the insurance terms are standard or customized, the parties will provide drafts of the construction documents to their insurance consultants, who will provide indications and certificates and other paperwork pertaining to insurance. However, it is a rare insurance consultant who will actually read the construction contract with any real understanding, and it is not likely that the lawyer or architect is going to review insurance policies to see if they line up with the insurance contract.

Bad coordination on the interface between the insurance consultants and the lawyers who write the contract can cost a great deal of money. For example, the standard form of construction contract published by the AIA states that the owner must obtain property insurance covering the work, including parts of the work anywhere in the world while in transit. If, however, the owner has obtained his property insurance using a standard commercial property insurance form, such as the CP 00 20 builders risk form published by the Insurance Services Office (ISO), then the insurance does not apply until materials and equipment and other parts of the work are delivered to the site or laid down within one hundred feet of the site. Now, if the contractor ordered a very large and expensive piece of equipment to be shipped by rail cross-country and it were lost in transit, the owner could be facing a claim due to its failure to maintain insurance. This exposure could have been avoided had the contract draftsperson been aware of the insurance program, and modified the contract to make it clear that owner insures the work only at the site. With that change in the contract, the contractor would have been on notice to obtain insurance on the shipment to cover it from the manufacturer's shipping dock until its arrival at the site (at which point the builders risk insurance would attach). And just because the builders risk is written as "Inland Marine" instead of commercial property does not always solve this problem: some IM policies cover the work anywhere in the world, but others exclude property that is not at or near the site. IM policies have to be read even more carefully because they are so variable.

Insurance "Wrap Up" Programs

There are many other points at which the terms of the construction contract should be coordinated with the insurance program. One recurrent set of issues concerns "insurance wrap-up programs." These programs provide insurance coverage for "all" of the contractors on a project, as well as the owner, and include general liability, workers compensation, and excess liability in one convenient package. The covered contractors contribute to the cost of the program through discounts in their rates for work or through more or less elaborate accounting-based systems. These programs generally carry sky-high limits of liability as well as substantial deductible or self-insured retention (SIR) amounts. The difference between these two concepts—deductible and SIR—is critically important. When insurance is subject to a deductible, the insurance company pays the injured party for the entire loss, and then recoups the deductible from the policyholder. When there is a SIR, the insurance company pays nothing until the policyholder has paid out the amount of the SIR: not even defense costs are covered until the policyholder has paid the SIR out of pocket.

Bid packages have been issued for billon-dollar-plus projects that required all trade contractors to enroll in a wrap that carried a million-dollar SIR. The net result was that the trade contractors would have been working without coverage for their defense costs. To make matters even more depressing, the SIR applied per occurrence, and most construction sites have multiple occurrences. There was a real prospect of losing the company by doing work on this monumental project. Of course, the enrollment package for the contractors made no mention of the magnitude of the SIR. When enough of the contractors balked, the insurance company miraculously unveiled a "deductible endorsement" that gave the trades the "first dollar" coverage that they needed.

The key to integrating the documents lies in actually reviewing them. If the lawyer is responsible for producing a contract for construction, it behooves the lawyer and his client for the lawyer actually to know what is in the contract. It also pays, when making representations about the content of a related contract—such as an insurance policy—for the drafter of the contract to have gathered the information necessary for him to know what he is talking and writing about.

That process of gathering and integrating information is invaluable in another way: it opens channels of communication. These channels may make it possible for counsel and his client to become aware of problems on the horizon, instead of waiting until the storm strikes. It also enables counsel to engage in the team building exercises that prove invaluable when a workable response to problems is needed. If counsel has produced an integrated contract that reflects the interests of all stakeholders, then half the battle is won: the parties are used to working together and with counsel, the contract holds more than a chance of being fair and balanced, and the contract will be a useful tool for resolving problems instead of an ongoing occasion for disputes and claims.

Key Takeaways

- Understand that the construction contract includes far more than the documents prepared by the attorney, and all are equally important.
- Work with project managers and insurance consultants to identify risks and select effective, economical solutions.
- Collaborative work during contract development will facilitate easier resolution of disputes that arise between your client and other parties.

Kevin J. Connolly is a shareholder in the New York City firm of Anderson Kill & Olick PC, where he directs the firm's transactional construction risk practice in addition to representing architects, engineers, owners, developers, constructors, and financiers. He has authored numerous works addressing the rights and responsibilities of participants in the construction process, with particular emphasis on the importance of the contract as a tool for sharing and allocating risks.

Dedication: *This chapter is dedicated to James P. Cullen, BG (US Army Res., Ret'd), who reminds us all that there is much more to the practice of law than making money.*

Tactics for Facilitating Successful Real Estate Transactions

Jane B. Morgan
Member
Watkins & Eager PLLC

ASPATORE

Introduction

Recently, the focus of my real estate practice has been on mixed use development projects, commercial real estate financing, workouts, and foreclosures. At its core, with a few notable exceptions such as flying fee and other air space cases, a real estate practice is about the "dirt" and every property is different, just like every person is different. When working on a real estate development, it is important for lawyers to visit the physical site of the project in order to appreciate the quirks and unique aspects of the landscape and to understand the developer's vision. One site visit can transform the drafting of project documents from the mere massaging of mundane forms into crafting legal agreements that actually translate the parties' intent for that piece of real estate.

It is important to never forget the basics. Time spent analyzing riparian rights or debating prescriptive easements with the elder statesmen of the real property bar is never wasted. We are most fortunate in our law firm to have several octogenarian lawyers. Suffice it to say that they have just about seen it all, and a lot can be learned from them. Although today's real estate lawyers are expected to be versant in everything from conduit financing to TIF bond deals, long-established (and sometimes archaic) state property law is at the core of our practice. For example, in the jurisdiction where I practice, our statutes provide for three types of conveyance deeds, commonly referred to as a warranty deed, a special warranty deed, and a quitclaim deed. If a seller is required in a real estate purchase contract to convey by warranty deed or general warranty deed, then the seller must warrant not only title but also all of the covenants known to common law, namely: seizin, power to sell, freedom from incumbrance, and quiet enjoyment. Miss. Code Ann. 89-1-33 (1972). In contrast, if the contract calls for a special warranty deed, the seller is entitled in the conveyance deed to "warrant specially," which is a lesser form of warranty. Instead of warranting the five common law covenants, the conveyance by special warranty deed permits the seller to "warrant specially," which means that the seller, his heirs and personal representatives only promise to warrant and defend title to the property against claims by any persons claiming through the seller. Miss. Code Ann. 89-1-35. Last in the hierarchy of conveyances is the quitclaim, which merely passes all the estate or interest that the seller has in the land—whatever that might be—but also estops the seller and his heirs from later asserting title by adverse possession to the sold property. Miss. Code Ann. 89-1-39. Anyone who buys property in our state and thinks he got the best deed possible just because it was labeled "special," might want to take some time to get back to basics before doing another real estate deal. That said, a special warranty deed may be perfectly acceptable in any given transaction and is commonly used in commercial real estate transactions depending on the business involved and the needs of the developer.

Although each real estate deal is different, my practice has led me to conclude that there are some basic principles common to all that revolve around proper preparation, good communication, document organization, and attention to detail.

Effective Practices for Commercial Real Estate Transactions

First and foremost, the lawyer's job is to listen to the client's evaluation and goals for the project. For example, if the client is a seasoned developer who arrives with a well-developed site plan and approved zoning letter for a traditional condominium development on a tract of land that the client already owns, then my job should be relatively streamlined and the client's legal costs can be kept to a minimum. At this stage, my primary functions might be limited to:

1. preparing a condominium declaration and covenants suitable to the project in proper form for recording;
2. working with the developer-client and engineer to produce a legally compliant and recordable condominium plat with all the proper certifications and notarized signatures required by the applicable governmental authorities;
3. recording the condominium documents; and
4. setting up the condominium association.

If, on the other hand, the client arrives with hopes of purchasing property that is tied up in a contested estate and wants to build a commercial office park, but has no idea how the property is currently zoned, then I immediately know that significant up-front leg work will be required of me and that the jury is out on whether this transaction will come to fruition. In an effort to keep initial legal costs under control, I would probably suggest that the client begin by contacting the proper governmental authorities to determine the current zoning of the property. If it is not already zoned commercial, then we will discuss the legal and political hoops, time delays, and attorney costs involved in changing the zoning designation. These uncertainties alone, not to mention the seller's ability to transfer clean title, might influence a purchaser to look for alternative sites.

Preparing Clients for Successful Real Estate Transactions

In every commercial real estate transaction, some basic items are generally needed: good title to the property, access, proper zoning, adequate parking, utilities, environmental assurances, flood plain information, and a financing commitment. I will make sure that the client has each of these covered, and if this is not the case, I will explore each more thoroughly with the client. I ask to see a survey because even an old survey is better than no survey at all in the initial stages. An updated survey will be required by the lender prior to closing. I want to know that the client has confirmed that the property site is suitable for the intended use before the client spends a lot of money on legal fees and development costs. I will also ask to see any drawings that an architect has done to date of the project.

Another item that should be dealt with early on is the structure of the transaction and whether new corporate entities will be needed to facilitate the transaction. For example, I will ask the client if a special purpose entity has been formed to serve as the "declarant" for purposes of the covenants in a condominium or subdivision project. I will need to know from the outset if the property is subject to any regulatory agreements (e.g., Land Use Restriction Agreements under Section 42 of the Internal Revenue Code) or is located in a Tax Increment Financing (TIF) District, Planned Unit Development (PUD), or a Public Improvement District (PID), which may require special disclosures in project documents (see example of PID disclosure below) and can result in taxes or assessments that the developer will need to address and budget, to the extent quantifiable. For example, the governing board of a PID district will determine PID assessments annually based on costs of public improvements and services. Such assessments are levied in addition to annual property taxes and should not be overlooked when budgeting project costs. Careful budgeting also is required for projects conducted in TIF districts. If properly authorized, a developer may qualify for reimbursement of certain infrastructure costs by the governmental issuer of TIF bonds, which may be issued once ad valorem and sales tax revenues in the TIF district reach sufficient levels to pay off the bonds. Because of the political and legal variables involved, budgeting for the expenditure of such costs and eventual reimbursement is far from an exact science.

Conducting Research

In any real estate transaction, the key piece of "research" will be the title search. At a closing, the lender will require a mortgagee's title insurance policy subject only, as a general rule, to taxes and assessments that are not yet due and payable, prior reservations or conveyances of minerals including oil, gas, sand, and gravel, and certain utility and other easements on a case-by-case basis. If the initial title search is not "clean," additional legal research will be required to correct the exceptions to title. Such research topics might include heirship and estate issues, adverse possession, and the elements of prescriptive easements, to name but a few. Easement research can prove critical if the only access to the property is by virtue of an easement and not by direct access to a public road. Uncertainty over access will make a commercial real estate deal ineligible for title insurance and financing, thereby killing the deal.

If the real property is located in a PID or other statutorily created area, legal research may be required to identify specific disclosures that need to be included in project documents. By way of example, in the state of Mississippi, a purchase agreement for property located in a PID must contain the following disclosure, boldfaced and in conspicuous type that is larger than the type in the rest of the contract:

> THE _____PUBLIC IMPROVEMENT DISTRICT MAY IMPOSE AND LEVY ASSESSMENTS ON THIS PROPERTY. THESE ASSESSMENTS PAY THE CONSTRUCTION, OPERATION AND MAINTENANCE COSTS OF CERTAIN PUBLIC FACILITIES AND SERVICES OF THE DISTRICT AND ARE SET ANNUALLY BY THE

GOVERNING BOARD OF THE DISTRICT. THESE ASSESSMENTS ARE IN ADDITION TO COUNTY AND OTHER LOCAL GOVERNMENTAL TAXES AND ASSESSMENTS AND ALL OTHER TAXES AND ASSESSMENTS PROVIDED FOR BY LAW.

Miss. Code Ann. 19-35-45. In short, the relevant jurisdiction's real property statutes should always be close at hand throughout the life of a real estate transaction, from the initial purchase through the recording of the last document and thereafter.

If the client has not already done the proper homework on the zoning of the property, legal and non-legal (i.e., political) research will be required. In cases where property must be rezoned for the project to go through, compliance with the legal requirements for rezoning may not be overwhelming, but satisfying the adjacent property owners, concerned citizens, and governmental authorities can be a deal killer. Non-legal research to take the temperature of potential opponents to the zoning change cannot be overlooked. This can be accomplished by polling the neighboring property owners. In some cases, the best approach may be to send out letters and post notices that invite the affected owners to a meeting. Such informal meetings give the client the opportunity to explain the project in a non-legal setting, present projections as to increased traffic, environmental impact, and other potential changes, and answer questions that those affected might have. In addition to polling the adjacent owners, the client will need supporters among the members of the governmental authority or authorities whom are authorized to approve or reject rezoning requests. This may require some networking and nonlegal research to figure out where any political opposition to the project might lie.

Other non-legal research on the front end of a real estate transaction might include the gathering of tax assessment information from the applicable taxing authorities, people searches for existing tenants or third parties whose consents might be required or desirable, and seeking referrals and recommendations so that the right team of engineers, surveyors, environmental consultants, and other service providers is assembled to make the closing happen in an efficient and timely manner. If a real estate broker is involved in the transaction, certain non-legal research such as targeting the correct market for advertising and marketing activities may be performed by the broker, provided these duties are covered in the real estate broker listing agreement.

Document Organization

There is a tremendous volume of real estate, corporate, financing, and other documents that may be included in a commercial real estate transaction. Many of these documents will be negotiated, revised, and exchanged electronically numerous times prior to closing. Particularly when a number of team members are working on the same transaction, it is essential in this age of electronic document exchange that a strict document control system is in place and that every team member is required to adhere to that system.

The Benefits of a Virtual Data Room

In large complex transactions, a virtual data room administered by a third party vendor may be the most desirable document control system. Unfortunately, this service comes with a price tag that is not realistic for the vast majority of transactions. Most transactions can be efficiently administered in-house by setting up a central folder on a computer network that contains every piece of paper related to the transaction (title documents, surveys, architectural drawings, contracts, financing documents and security agreements, correspondence, memoranda, invoices, etc.). A standard coding system that identifies the category of document and the chronological sequence of contract drafts must be established and adhered to by all. As new documents and drafts arrive, they must be promptly stored in electronic format or scanned and stored in the central folder. As morbid as this may sound, the goal for a document control system must be that, even if everyone working on the transaction died, a legal team unrelated to the transaction could nonetheless step in and pick up where the first team left off.

Preparing Documents

The documents that I prepare depend entirely on whom I am representing, the precise type of commercial real estate transaction involved, at what stage I enter into the transaction, and any unique property-specific issues associated with the land being acquired and/or developed. In general, if I am representing the developer or borrower in the transaction, I will likely prepare the real estate purchase contract if the land has not yet been acquired. In the initial purchase transaction, I may prepare (or the seller's attorney will prepare for my review and comment) release documents to remove existing liens and mortgages, various assignments of easements and other rights, title insurance policy, owner's and contractor's affidavit, FIRPTA affidavit, assumption agreement if the mortgage or deed of trust is to be assumed, closing statement, and other documents typical to the specific type of transaction (e.g., tenant estoppel certificates if a shopping center is being purchased, lease assignments, etc.). As a general rule in the jurisdiction where I practice, the seller's attorney will prepare the deed (warranty, special or quitclaim) and other documents necessary to convey title and grant property rights.

In the development phase of the real estate project, the documents that I prepare as developer's counsel will depend wholly on the type of commercial real estate transaction involved. For example, in a simple office park condominium development, I would work with the developer to craft a Declaration of Covenants, Restrictions and Conditions suited for the particular development and recordable under applicable law. I would prepare formation documents, resolutions, and corporate authority documents for the condominium association and declarant/developer, including bylaws. If there are to be multiple office condominiums in one office park, then I will likely need to prepare a master set of covenants to "umbrella" the entire development.

Representing a Lender

If I am representing the lender in a commercial real estate transaction, the typical list of financing documents that the lender's counsel will be called upon to prepare may include the following: commitment letter, promissory note, loan agreement, mortgage or deed of trust (depending on the jurisdiction), leasehold mortgage (if applicable), security agreement, assignment of rents and leases, other collateral security documents, UCC financing statements, guaranties, estoppel certificates, SNDA (subordination, nondisturbance and attornment agreement), environmental indemnification agreement, form of opinion of borrower's counsel, certifications from various third parties such as the surveyor and architect, other affidavits and certifications related to property-specific or borrower-specific matters, intercreditor agreement if mezzanine financing is involved, and a closing checklist—the key to making sure that all documents are on track and stay on track until closing. A sample closing checklist for a real estate financing transaction is included as Appendix K. Of all of the foregoing transactional documents, the cornerstone of most commercial real estate financing transactions will be the mortgage or deed of trust.

Because all of the above-listed documents may go through numerous drafts at a rapid pace before a final, execution copy is agreed upon by the parties, it is imperative to establish a strict document control system from beginning to end of any real estate transaction.

Filing Deadlines

Filing deadlines are entirely dependent on what type of transaction is at issue. The mortgage or deed of trust and all other recordable documents should be recorded as soon as possible upon closing of the transaction to avoid intervening lien attachment. Other deadlines may be driven by construction schedules, funding availability or marketing opportunities.

A specific type of real estate transaction with explicit and unforgivable deadlines is the 1031 exchange. The basic deadlines in a traditional 1031 transaction are:

1. The property to be received in exchange must be identified on or before the forty-fifth day after the original property is transferred
2. The 1031 exchange must be completed within the earliest of (x) 180 days of the transfer or (y) the due date for the taxpayer's tax return for the year in which the transfer occurs.

In other words, if the due date for the current year tax return falls before the expiration of the 180-day period, then the exchange must be closed on or before the tax return due date.

Creating New Construction Loans and Real Estate Transactions

Most construction financing is short term and at higher interest rates than permanent financing because of the risk that the construction may not be completed. I generally advise clients to get bids for a take-out commitment, which is a commitment to "flip" from construction to permanent financing once construction is completed to the lender's satisfaction and other preconditions to conversion are satisfied. Some of the classic preconditions that many lenders require before a construction loan can be converted to a permanent term loan include, among others:

- Giving the lender thirty days or longer prior written notice of the proposed conversion date
- Substantial completion of the project in accordance with the plans and specifications that were approved by the lender
- Evidence that all costs for labor and materials incurred in the construction have been paid and that no mechanic's, materialman's, or other statutory liens have been filed against the project
- Evidence that all insurance policies required by the lender are in full force and effect
- Satisfaction of certain financial covenants established by the lender such as achievement for a certain number of consecutive months of a specific debt service coverage ratio
- Achievement of occupancy percentages set by the lender (typically seen, for example, in apartment complex projects and retail shopping center projects) at projected rental rates
- Providing the lender with endorsements to the mortgagee's title insurance policy
- Payment or reimbursement for all the lender's expenses and costs, including attorneys' fees and disbursements
- No defaults under the existing loan documents
- The lender's inspecting architect must have issued a Certificate of Completion
- Delivery of a permanent certificate of occupancy from all necessary governmental authorities
- Receipt of a final as-built survey for the project acceptable to the lender and the title insurance company, which shows the total square footage and dimensions, access to the property, the location of all improvements, boundaries, encroachments, setback lines, rights of ways and easements

Wrapping the construction and permanent financing into one loan agreement and one closing can often save costs for the client.

Steps to Success in New Construction Loans and Real Estate Transactions

Apart from the normal real estate acquisition steps (i.e., confirm good title, confirm proper zoning, obtain an environmental audit, have a survey completed, etc.), a fundamental step is to make sure that the plans and specifications are complete, comply with all local building codes, zoning ordinances and other local restrictions, and are satisfactory to the lender. The plans and specifications will typically be incorporated into the construction contract, which, in many cases, will be based on the American Institute of Architects (AIA) form. The construction loan cannot close, until the construction contract and plans and specifications are final and approved by the lender or the lender's architect.

The client will need to pick the contractor with care and ensure that the contractor is financially viable and able to complete the work on time. The lender will likely require payment and performance bonds, which the client should, in turn, require of the contractor.

Other construction issues that the client needs to consider and include in the construction contract are retention amounts, requirements that the contractor carry sufficient liability and builder's risk insurance that covers both the contractor and client, and covenants by the contractor to comply with all applicable laws including, for example, permitting and building inspection ordinances, environmental laws, and state and federal safety rules.

Working with Third Parties

The key people involved in construction loans and real estate transactions are the borrower's architect and contractor, and the lender's inspecting architect. On smaller loans, some lenders will permit the borrower's architect to certify to the lender when construction milestones are completed. On large construction loans, lenders generally will insist on hiring their own architect or construction expert to inspect the work and either approve it or report on any corrections needed before a construction draw can be funded.

The contractor is responsible for completing the work according to the plans and specifications and for hitting construction milestones in accordance with the construction contract in a timely and professional manner. The borrower's architect will supervise and ensure that the project is being completed according to the plans and specifications that were approved by the lender. The borrower's architect will sign off on the work as it is completed and coordinate the timing of inspections that are conducted by the lender's inspecting architect.

When working with architects and contractors, it is imperative that the client stay on top of the construction progress. A good approach on some jobs is for the client to name a point person within the client's organization, preferably someone with construction and/or architectural experience. This point person (or "owner's representative" under the typical AIA construction contract) will need to visit the site on a regular basis with the architect and the contractor's project manager in order to identify any problems before it is too late in the game to correct errors or make changes. Variations in the plans and specifications will need to be reported to and approved by the lender and its inspecting architect.

Representing Clients Selling to Commercial Developers

When representing a client selling to a commercial developer, I try to help the client to focus on issues often associated with the sale of raw land. The key issues for a client selling "raw land" to a commercial developer typically will be providing clean title, making sure there are no access problems, making it clear that the client provides no environmental representations or indemnities and no representations as to the property's suitability for any specific purpose, and settling on a price that is at least as good as recent, comparable sales in the area. All of these items, and others peculiar to the property, should be handled in the sales contract. Any restrictions that are to run with the land should be expressly included in the sales contract, and the buyer should acknowledge in the sales contract that the restrictions would be included in the deed or other document of conveyance.

I negotiate as many or as few selling terms for my client as the client desires. However, the client always has the final say on the entire package and, without exception, on price. Much depends on the sophistication of the client and sometimes on the time that the client has to invest in negotiating terms without lawyer assistance. I most always find it preferable to draft the sales agreement myself rather than have the client use a broker's form. For expediency and to save costs, many clients want to use a real estate broker's contract rather than pay an attorney to do the drafting. In some cases, the form contract will suffice. However, in deals that have unique aspects such as peculiar deadlines, financing requirements, and inspection or environmental issues, a custom-drafted contract can save money and alleviate arguments on the back end.

The Components of the Sales Agreement

The sales agreement includes some basic provisions that are part of every sales agreement. These include the parties' names and legal status, property description, title requirements, purchase price, deposit requirements, payment requirements, various inspections and the time frame to complete them, disclosures legally necessary or advisable, the allocation of closing costs (including recording fees), proration of taxes, default remedies, and closing requirements such as deadlines, time, and place.

Each deal may require variations on those basic provisions or may also require tailor-made provisions applicable to that specific transaction. For example, with respect to the purchase price, the price may be fixed, it may be a price per acre subject to a final survey of the property, or it may depend on the number of units eventually allowed under a sought-after zoning change. The price per acre may vary depending on the topography of the land (i.e., flood plain land would be sold at a lesser price per acre), or the price can vary depending on when parcels from a large tract of land are released to the seller, if the takeout of parcels is scheduled over a period of time.

If the seller is retaining portions of the adjacent or surrounding property, then the seller may wish to include in the purchase contract reasonable restrictions on the use or development of the sold property. Such restrictions also should be included in recorded covenants that govern the use of a defined area of land. Any such restrictions will need to pass legal muster under local law and should be reviewed carefully. As a general rule, courts "favor free and unobstructed use of real property." *Kinchen v. Layton*, 457 So.2d 343, 345 (Miss. 1984). Nonetheless, clearly and unambiguously drafted covenants may be enforced; ambiguously drafted covenants will be subject to a court's strict scrutiny and will be construed against the person seeking enforcement of the covenant. *Id.* (prefabricated home that was mounted on masonry peers was not a "temporary structure" prohibited by restrictive land-use covenants on the real property).

The Role of Commercial Lenders

As a lawyer, I am governed by the rules of professional responsibility, which require that I deal directly with the lender's lawyer and not directly with the bank officer in charge. That is not to say that I never speak to the lender. All-hands meetings and conference calls, where the lender and its counsel are present, are often helpful and necessary in moving a deal along. As a general rule, I try to keep good lines of communication open with lender's counsel at all times. The use of e-mail has certainly improved the ability to communicate with opposing counsel rapidly and has eliminated many problems associated with phone tag in the past.

Lenders and Structuring the Transaction

Lenders will always have the final say on the transaction's structure, particularly from the standpoint of what collateral must be pledged and from whom, what personal and/or corporate guaranties will be required, whether special purpose entities (SPEs) will need to be formed and how, and with respect to funding amounts and timing. Simply put, if a lender is not comfortable with the structure of the transaction, the deal is dead.

Recently enacted financial reform legislation is expected by some to have a negative impact on lending to commercial real estate markets. The Dodd-Frank Wall Street Reform and Consumer Protection Act, signed by President Obama on July 21, 2010 as Public Law No: 111-203, has been described as the most sweeping regulation of financial services in this country since the New Deal Programs were enacted in response to the Great Depression. Even though the Dodd-Frank Act arguably has a more direct and immediate impact on consumer mortgage financing (by virtue of the creation of the Consumer Financial Protection Bureau) than on commercial real estate transactions, financial reform has tightened capital and compliance requirements on banks, which, in turn, has slowed the underwriting process for commercial lending and made the process more onerous for potential borrowers. Additionally, Dodd-Frank has imposed greater disclosure requirements on issuers of commercial mortgage-backed securities and further has required that issuers retain no less than a 5 percent unhedged economic interest in the securitized assets that they transfer. Some observers expect these added layers of regulation to contribute to an even more restrictive commercial lending market than what we currently have.

Whether or not the cause is directly or indirectly attributable to Dodd-Frank, commercial real estate lenders are proceeding cautiously and are "kicking the tires" more thoroughly than in past years. In some areas, the process has slowed to a standstill. The general rule of thumb now is that a borrower/developer must present to the lender thorough project plans, budgets, and analyses in order to win approval from the typical loan committee or investor group.

Organizing Commercial Real Estate Documents

Document drafts for commercial real estate transactions are generated in electronic format and then distributed by e-mail to all parties involved for review and comment. Once all comments are received and discussed with the client, new drafts are generated and distributed in "clean" and "black lined" versions, which show all changes from the prior drafts. This process will continue until final, execution copies are agreed upon.

The basic information needed to begin drafting real estate transaction documents includes true and correct names and addresses of the parties involved, corporate formation information, all information needed to prepare statutorily correct notarial acknowledgments in the relevant jurisdiction (e.g., in Mississippi, one must know whether limited liability companies are member-managed or manager-managed), proper legal descriptions, an accurate survey, a current title report with copies of the documents listed in the report, a zoning letter to confirm zoning representations, and any deal-specific information required for a particular transaction. In the drafting of bank documents, the lawyer needs the signed loan commitment in order to commence document preparation.

The primary challenge involved in real estate transactions is usually timing. Parties generally wish to close yesterday. Clean title, access, zoning, and permitting issues can slow down the process tremendously. These types of problems are overcome with patience, hard work, and sometimes, luck.

Tax Considerations and Closings

Some of the basic tax considerations are the recognition of gain or loss and opportunities to defer gain. A Section 1031 like-kind exchange, mentioned above, is a common vehicle for avoiding the recognition of gain in a real estate transaction. Other tax driven opportunities should be considered such as GO Zone bond financing and other tax incentives, which became available in the states of Louisiana, Mississippi, and Alabama after the devastation of Hurricanes Katrina and Rita in 2005. Congress recently extended, and President Obama signed into law, certain GO Zone tax incentives, which were originally enacted following the devastation of Hurricanes Katrina and Rita on the Gulf Coast in 2005. The centerpiece of the hurricane relief contained in the Gulf Opportunity Zone Act of 2005 (Public Law No: 109-135) was a package of tax incentives designed to help revitalize and rebuild the areas hardest hit (aka "the GO Zone") by Hurricanes Katrina and Rita. The federal tax benefits that were made available to businesses under the GO Zone legislation included 50 percent bonus first-year depreciation, a nearly doubled Code Section 179 expensing allowance, partial expensing of demolition and cleanup costs, a five-year-NOL carryback, and increased rehabilitation tax credits.

Approaching Complex Tax Issues and Closing Commercial Real Estate Loans

Because I am not a tax lawyer, I often work with the client's accountant to ensure that a transaction is structured in a tax efficient manner that complies with the accountant's overall goals for the particular client. Certain transactions may be dependent on Internal Revenue Code (the Code) provisions, such as low-income housing projects under Section 42 of the Code or the rehabilitation of certified historic structures under Code

Section 47, and will require the hands-on involvement of the client's tax accountant or advisor. The tax professional will be called upon to render tax compliance certifications to the lender and investors and to fulfill reporting requirements to the IRS.

In every commercial real estate financing transaction, I always create a closing checklist from the very beginning of the transaction so that each party knows what everyone is required to bring to the table and when. The closing checklist can often be the most important document in the transaction.

Construction, Permanent, and Mezzanine Loans

All parties including the developer, lender, contractor, architect, and lawyers, must work together on a strict timetable when working to create a successful construction loan. They must also be flexible enough to deal with unique problems as they arise, and timing is key. Weather is the classic and uncontrollable variable that can play havoc with the best-planned construction schedules. Labor and supply shortages (e.g., sheetrock shortage during the building boom of 2004 to 2006, which lead to the Chinese drywall problems being litigated today) also can cause deviations from the schedule. Construction and development projects must be properly permitted, and approvals from governmental authorities often take longer to obtain than anticipated.

Construction and permanent financing may be wrapped into one takeout commitment. If structured in this manner, the flip to permanent financing should not require a "second" closing but can be streamlined to satisfying the lender that completion requirements have been met. With respect to mezzanine financing, such loans are typically large loans that are highly paperwork intensive and primarily seen on larger projects. Mezzanine loans are supplementary financing and are analogous to second mortgages, but the collateral for the mezzanine loan is the equity ownership interests (stock or limited liability company membership interests) of the owner of the real property rather than the property itself. Organized due diligence and document control is key when closing a mezzanine loan as part of a real estate financing transaction.

Conclusion

Since being struck by the financial crisis that spawned legislation such as Dodd-Frank, the commercial real estate market has gone through a serious decline; experts are now arguing over whether we have seen the bottom or whether further decline is in store. In our practice, we have seen some recent increase in activity, but I think it is fair to say that, in the first quarter of 2011, the commercial real estate market remains anemic. While there are some signs that fuel optimism such as statistics that show an increase in Real Estate Investment Trust (REIT) annual returns and some perceived easing in the underwriting standards for commercial loans, there still are difficult problems on the horizon. Primary among these concerns is the spike in commercial real estate debt maturities that is predicted to be in the $350 billion range from 2011 through 2013. *See* testimony of Matthew J. Anderson, Managing Director of Foresight Analytics, before the Congressional Oversight Panel Hearing on Commercial Real Estate's Impact on Bank Stability, Washington, D.C. (Feb. 4, 2011) (website links for oral testimony and written research: http://cop.senate.gov/documents/testimony-020411-anderson.pdf; http://cop.senate.gov/documents/testimony-020411-anderson-oral.pdf)

There is no question that we still have difficult times ahead. The best advice to transactional real estate practitioners might be simply to remain patient—depressed prices should eventually translate into increased activity, including an increase in foreign investment. In the meantime, dirt lawyers who find themselves absent from the closing table can always bone up on foreclosure and workout skills, which, in these difficult financial times, seem likely to remain in demand.

Key Takeaways

- Complete the necessary legal and non-legal zoning research on properties if the client has not already done so.
- Consider using a virtual data room administered by a third party vendor in order to organize large complex transactions.
- Keep in mind that the client always has the final say on the entire package, even when the lawyer conducts the negotiations.

- Collaborate with financial advisors if you are dealing with complicated tax issues that you are not familiar with in order to ensure that the real estate transaction is financially secure and proper.
- Make sure that lines of communication with lenders are open and healthy so that you and your client will be more likely to have successful transactions.

Related Resources

- American Bankers Association Dodd-Frank Tracker: http://regreformtracker.aba.com/p/dodd-frank-tracker-topics-list.html
- Gulf Opportunity Zone Bonds, IRC ' 1400N(a): http://www.irs.gov/taxexemptbond/article/0,,id=155664,00.html

Jane B. Morgan is a member of Watkins & Eager PLLC in Jackson, Mississippi. After graduating with honors from the Georgetown University Law Center, she served as law clerk to the Honorable E. Grady Jolly of the United States Fifth Circuit Court of Appeals. Ms. Morgan was admitted to the bars of Pennsylvania, the District of Columbia, New York, Louisiana, and Mississippi, and now practices exclusively in Mississippi. Ms. Morgan regularly serves as Mississippi counsel and local opinion counsel in complex transactions that involve Mississippi real estate. Ms. Morgan has been named a "Mid-South Super Lawyer" and has received Martindale-Hubbell's "AV" peer rating.

Implementing Successful Commercial Real Estate Strategies

Kwame A. Benjamin
Partner
Seyfarth Shaw LLP

ASPATORE

Introduction

Within my practice, I handle most matters related to commercial real estate, including acquisition and disposition transactions, but I tend to focus on commercial real estate development, including multi-family and retail development transactions, and office, industrial, and retail leasing matters.

I assume that all good commercial real estate attorneys focus on effectively representing their clients' interests in order to close transactions, but what makes my approach most effective is that I also strive to understand the clients' business goals for a transaction, to provide practical advice and counsel before, during, and after the transaction has closed, and to efficiently close the transaction in the most cost-effective manner. At the outset of a transaction, I discuss the client's needs and expectations for the transaction as well as the client's plans for the real property asset after closing has occurred. This approach includes focusing on strategies to most efficiently structure and close the deal; identifying and addressing lead time items that should be resolved early in a deal's life span; identifying and addressing any operational issues related to the real property asset; and contemplating and discussing transaction and property-related issues on which lenders, investors, or prospective end users may focus.

By reviewing and discussing a transaction as a whole with the client, and considering the client's intended end result for the transaction and plans for the asset, all parties to a transaction benefit by having a "road map" to the shared goal of a successful and issue-free closing and, thereafter, minimal or no issues during ownership, financing, and disposition of the asset. This approach is especially beneficial during acquisition and development transactions for which it is of the utmost importance that development and property issues, and lead-time items, be quickly raised, addressed, and resolved so that unexpected costs of the transaction can be identified as soon as possible and transaction pursuit costs and risks can be minimized.

The Current Trends in Commercial Real Estate Development

At present, commercial real estate development has been limited due to the difficulties in the national and global economy. New developments have been placed on hold or have not commenced due to the lack of end users as well as difficulties obtaining affordable financing for the acquisition and development of properties. However, there are some development "bright spots." It appears that the volume of multi-family apartment developments is increasing. As a result of more stringent underwriting requirements for single family home mortgages, the rental market has remained stable, if not expanded. In addition, although construction and development lenders appear more willing to consider projects and make traditional loans to multi-family developers, special financing opportunities, such as through the US Department of Housing and Urban Development's (HUD) Section 221(d)(4) loan program, have permitted multi-family projects to continue to be developed. The HUD Section 221(d)(4) program facilitates construction and development loans for qualifying multi-family apartment projects by guaranteeing the loans at 90 percent of the replacement cost of the projects, thereby limiting the risk to lenders issuing these loans. In addition, outparcel development transactions, including transactions on behalf of the operators of casual dining and fast-food restaurants, appear to have remained stable. Operators focused on pursuing expansion opportunities have benefited from depressed real estate prices and the interest of property owners in disposing of or generating revenue from excess property.

One of the most recent developments in commercial real estate transactions is the focus on sustainability or "green" transactions. Primarily based on the certification system promulgated by the United States Green Building Council and commonly known as LEED (Leadership in Energy and Environmental Design), commercial tenants are requiring that leased space and buildings meet certain sustainability thresholds, and landlords are utilizing LEED certification to attract tenants and to market space and buildings. In addition to the focus on sustainability issues by developers, landlords, and tenants, lenders will need to be more attentive to sustainability requirements related to commercial real estate that they finance—ranging from a focus on the requirements of tenants who have leased or intend to lease space in the collateral property, to sustainability requirements of the governmental agencies approving new development projects. Governmental entities are "suggesting" that certain green measures be included in new developments as a condition to providing site plan and project approval, but it is anticipated that statutes and ordinances requiring sustainability thresholds and establishing certain sustainability requirements for new developments and commercial property rehabilitation projects will become more common. A careful review of the local jurisdiction's sustainability requirements and laws should be performed with respect to any new real estate project.

Although development transactions have been limited, the current trend in commercial real estate transactions appears to be focused on the disposition and acquisition of income producing properties. From multi-family properties to office properties, assets with stabilized occupancies have been attractive to investors. Many investment funds have been formed over the past few years to pursue and acquire so-called distressed assets at a discount, and these funds have cash to invest as equity in transactions or to acquire assets without financing. At the same time, the developers and owners of income producing assets have been interested in disposing of the assets—either the asset is truly distressed and is on the verge of foreclosure by the owner's lender and satisfactory permanent or "take-out" financing is unavailable, or the owner's loan has been foreclosed and the property is owned by the lender who intends to dispose of the collateral.

The Attorney's Role in Assembling Commercial Real Estate Transactions

The role of attorneys in structuring a real estate transaction is to listen to their clients and understand the clients' needs and goals for real estate transactions. This conversation must occur at the outset of a transaction and, preferably, before or during the client's negotiation of business terms with the other party and the preparation of a letter of intent. Considerations related to timing of the transaction, financing, the performance of diligence, and the client's ultimate use and disposition of the property asset should be discussed with the client. An informed approach to the transaction permits the attorney to focus on the most critical issues when drafting and negotiating the purchase and sale agreement, so that any necessary development agreements or ancillary property agreements can be addressed with the other party early in the transaction—such as easements, covenants, and restrictions—and to be proactive with respect to issues that will likely be raised by lenders.

During the last few years, this role has become even more important. With respect to development and acquisition transactions, clients are more interested in minimizing costs and expenses for transactions, and want to limit pursuit costs and expenses for transactions that the clients will not ultimately close. As such, with more frequency, clients are requesting diligence items from the seller or pursuing the right to perform property diligence prior to the execution of a purchase and sale agreement. In these instances, an early access agreement is signed by both parties allowing the purchaser to enter the property in order to conduct site inspections. See Appendix M for a sample early access agreement. In addition, clients are engaging the planning department of the applicable jurisdiction to discuss process requirements and timing for the issuance of permits and approvals earlier in the transaction, and presenting conceptual plans for projects for initial comments. As a member of the client's development team, the successful attorney should drive the initial conversations regarding the project, assist with the drafting and negotiation of early access agreements and confidentiality agreements permitting the performance of property diligence prior to execution of the purchase contract, assist with the diligence reviews, and promptly counsel the client if any issues arise that may constitute an unforeseen cost for the client.

Strategies for Constructing Commercial Real Estate Transactions

Meeting with the Client

When structuring a commercial real estate development transaction, the first step in my process is to coordinate a conference with the client to discuss all aspects of the project, including a review of any property and project specific matters, the end use and operation of the property, the development process and required approvals in the applicable jurisdiction, and the business terms or contemplated business terms of the transaction. I also identify the client's project development team.

Once a letter of intent has been finalized and the purchase and sale agreement is being drafted and negotiated, dependent upon the client's timing and needs, an early access agreement will be presented to the seller party with the intent of promptly commencing site diligence inspections. Upon execution of the purchase and sale agreement, assuming that the client is genuinely interested in pursuing the project and willing to incur additional pursuit costs, title and survey orders are initiated.

Putting Together an Acquisition and Development Transaction Checklist

With respect to all transactions, a timeline of critical dates should be prepared and discussed with the client, and the key transaction dates should be calendared to insure that the project is proceeding as planned. Similarly, a transaction checklist should be prepared listing standard transaction items to be addressed along with deal-specific matters discussed with the client and its development team during the initial conversations regarding the project. The transaction checklist should be routinely reviewed, discussed with the client, and updated in light of the critical dates for the transaction. See Appendix N for a sample transaction checklist.

Completing a New Construction Loan

When assisting a client as the borrower of a new construction loan, as with all real estate transactions, the first task is to conference with the client to discuss the specific terms of the loan set forth in the loan term sheet. Promptly after this initial background discussion with the borrower client, a conference call with the lender, borrower client, and the attorney representing the lender should be scheduled. This introductory conference call is critical to address any issues or questions that any party may have with respect to the loan transaction and deal terms, to discuss the asset or the status of the project to be financed, to discuss any diligence items that should be delivered to the lender and its counsel, and to set and understand the expectations of all parties to the transaction. During such calls, in addition to requesting an estimated delivery time for the loan documents being prepared by the lender's attorney, I request that a loan transaction checklist be prepared and delivered by the lender's attorney. Requesting and receiving such a checklist early in the loan transaction forces the lender and its attorney to review the transaction as a whole and the diligence and other items that the lender will require to efficiently close the loan transaction. Although issues may subsequently arise, the use of the loan transaction checklist should assist with tracking the loan to closing.

Once loan documents are delivered, they should be promptly reviewed and, to the extent any issues require input from the borrower client, a discussion with the client should occur. When time permits, I usually itemize the issues in a written correspondence to the client with proposed resolutions or positions for the client to consider. In my experience, this approach permits the client to review and ponder the issues and the proposed resolutions prior to any conference call regarding those matters, and, to the extent that a conference call is necessary, the matters can be efficiently discussed to minimize cost to the client. However, an important consideration prior to the review of loan documents for a transaction and any discussion of issues with the borrower client is whether the lender has previously made a loan to the borrower client. In such a case, while the loan documents for the current transaction must be thoroughly reviewed, the review and completion of the new loan documents may be more efficiently performed by reviewing the loan documents for the prior transaction, determining those matters that presented issues for the borrower client, and how those matters were satisfactorily resolved for the borrower client.

Throughout the real estate loan transaction, counsel for the borrower should be in routine contact with the lender's attorney to review the loan closing checklist, to discuss open matters, and to otherwise insure that the transaction is proceeding to closing in the most efficient manner. Since borrowers are typically responsible for the legal fees of the lender's counsel, proactively driving the loan transaction on behalf of a borrower client is critical to minimizing costs for the borrower client and avoiding any unexpected issues that may delay closing of the loan transaction and any related transaction that requires the loan financing.

The Importance of Understanding the Property Development Process

In addition to the standard matters that must be addressed and the diligence that must be reviewed and approved in connection with the acquisition of real property, property development transactions require a thorough understanding of the permitting and approval process for the jurisdiction in which the property is located and familiarity with the planned operation and uses of the proposed development. Working collaboratively with the client, the various departments, committees, and approval authorities in the applicable jurisdiction must be identified early in the process, and the requisite process for approvals permitting the development must be understood by the developer client. In connection with understanding the process for approvals, attention must be paid to the timing for the issuance of all permits and approvals. A firm understanding of the process and timing will benefit the developer client when negotiating diligence and approval time frames with the seller of the property.

In today's world, property sellers appear to be more anxious than ever to move as quickly as possible to closing the sale of the real property and, usually, the payoff of the seller's mortgage loan secured by the property. In such cases, the developer client's ability to provide a timeline to the seller describing the approval process and the necessary permits and approvals constitutes a strong basis for any request for extended time periods to close the transaction or before earnest money becomes non-refundable to the developer client.

Although a standard component of the permit and approval process, conditions imposed by jurisdictions remain a challenge for development transactions. In addition to typical site plan approval conditions such as landscaping requirements, some jurisdictions are requiring more extensive improvements such as the use of higher end materials and finishes, and the installation of acceleration lanes, deceleration lanes, and traffic signals. These requirements may result in unforeseen costs. Also, some jurisdictions are proposing the incorporation of sustainability measures for new development projects which may result in additional and unbudgeted costs for the developer client. Again, an early understanding of the approval process and engagement of the jurisdiction's officials will allow the developer client to identify potential requirements and properly budget and allocate costs to address such requirements.

Understanding the operation and use of the property to be developed is of critical importance in development transactions. Counsel for the developer should become intimately familiar with the preliminary site plan for the project, all revisions to the site plan, and the final site plan approved by the jurisdiction. Among other matters, counsel must understand how and where the improved property will be served with utility and drainage lines, whether the development will require any slope or lateral support from adjacent properties, whether any signage is necessary and where signage will be located, how the development will be accessed from adjacent rights-of-way and the resulting impact of traffic patterns and the parking layout on the property, and if any easements encumbering adjacent parcels will be necessary to facilitate the development and use of the property and address the aforementioned issues. Promptly focusing on and addressing these issues typically results in a more efficient land acquisition closing process and loan closing process, and prevents the need for a future request to the seller or adjacent property owners who would benefit from a position of leverage in any such request for an easement.

As a best practice, I counsel clients to always either incorporate sufficient time periods in the purchase and sale transaction for permits and approvals to be obtained, including any applicable appeal periods, before any or significant amounts of earnest money become non-refundable, or to require that issuance of the grading permit, land disturbance permit, or similar permit constituting the developer client's right to immediately commence construction and development activities is a contingency to the developer client's obligation to close or lose its earnest money. A sample purchase and sale agreement with such provisions, as well as standard purchase and sale agreement provisions, is included in Appendix O. Also, dependent upon the jurisdiction, it may be necessary to engage local land use counsel and local permitting consultants early in the transaction to assist with navigating the local permit process and building support for the project with neighboring communities. Although engaging these professionals may result in additional expenses, a thorough understanding of a jurisdiction's permitting process, including any politics involved in the process, will allow the developer client to sufficiently budget for these costs.

Finally, property development transactions require an understanding of how the land will actually be developed. Will the seller or a third party be required to perform any work? Where will construction materials and equipment be staged and stored during development of the property and the construction of improvements? With respect to these issues, will any costs be paid to a third party or due from a third party? A site development agreement is typically negotiated and executed to address the development of the property and any work performed by third parties or costs to be contributed by the developer or the third party. In addition to accurately itemizing and describing all site work to be performed, identifying who will perform the work, and setting forth a schedule for the completion of the work, a site development agreement should address lien rights on the property of the party for whom site development work has been performed, as well as self-help rights so that the party requiring the performance of the site development work can insure that all necessary work is timely completed.

Building a Knowledgeable and Cooperative Team

The key to successful development transactions is working with a knowledgeable and cooperative development team. The team typically consists of the development partner or project manager representing the owner, an architect who prepares conceptual site plans, specifications, and elevations for the project, an engineer, who, in collaboration with the architect, prepares engineering drawings and specifications for the project necessary for the pursuit of permits and approvals, and a local land use attorney to assist with permits, approvals, and zoning needs. In addition, a local permitting consultant may be necessary to lobby on behalf of the project with governmental officials and neighboring property owners. Similar to the land use attorney, in most cases, an engineer based in or near the jurisdiction of the project provides invaluable insight into the local development process and requirements, and usually has relationships with officials from the jurisdiction that may be beneficial in garnering support for the planned development. The owner should quickly identify and engage the professionals, and, after initial discussions with each regarding the project and the initial conceptual site plan, the owner should arrange a preliminary call to discuss the project with the entire team. In my experience, the most successful and streamlined development transactions have involved teams of professionals who routinely interact and discuss the status of the project.

Measuring Effectiveness and Success

With respect to real property development transactions, my metrics to evaluate success are:

1. Was the transaction timely closed and did development and construction activities commence as planned?
2. Did any unexpected issues arise, and if so, how many? Could those issues have been identified earlier in the transaction?
3. Were the budgeted costs of the client met, including the cost for legal services?

A transaction that timely closes and for which construction commences as planned will usually result in timely completion of the project for the client. Once completed, the asset can, hopefully, begin to generate income for the client, permit the client to refinance its construction and development loan with a more permanent, longer amortizing and non-recourse loan, or sell the asset.

While focusing on unexpected issues that arose during the development transaction provides a learning opportunity to all members of the development team, dependent upon the nature of the issue, I believe it demonstrates the level of engagement of the professionals involved with the project. Clearly, these matters should be identified and addressed as soon as possible to avoid any risks to or delays in the completion of the project and increased costs to the developer client. In light of costs, effectively communicating throughout the transaction, proactively focusing on the processes and steps necessary to close the acquisition and any financing, and insuring that the appropriate service provider is performing tasks at the appropriate rate, will result in the most cost-effective transaction for the developer client.

Market Innovations

With respect to routine transactions, Seyfarth Shaw LLP has become an innovator in the legal market by developing and deploying a product called "SeyfarthLean" which provides project mapping and process management. SeyfarthLean leads to a better understanding of the transaction process and, thus, drives more efficient transactions that typically result in lower costs for clients. As development activities continue to increase, we look forward to working with existing and new clients to continue to drive down costs for their real estate transactions.

Conclusion

All members of a transaction team should focus on thoroughly understanding the transaction, the necessary steps and processes to close the transaction, and the client's primary goals. Based on that understanding, a strategy for effectively executing the transaction should be prepared and discussed with the team. It is essential that the team members provide constant updates and communicate regarding issues related to the transaction. However, the attorney involved in the transaction should always seek to drive the team and the transaction toward closing. A lackadaisical approach to the transaction may result in increased costs for the client or, in the worst case, an unsuccessful transaction that cannot be closed or a project that cannot move forward.

Key Takeaways

- Listen to your clients and understand their needs and goals.
- Coordinate an initial team meeting, discuss the client's needs and expectations for the transaction and plans for the property post-closing.
- Identify who should perform which tasks and establish deadlines for completion.
- Identify all permits and approvals necessary for the project, and understand the process and timing to obtain those permits and approvals.
- Consider and discuss with the team any conditions to permits and approvals, including any sustainability requirements.
- Review sustainability laws and ordinances in the jurisdiction in which the real estate project is located.
- Identify and raise any deal-specific issues that may result in increased transaction costs for the client.
- Drive conversations with opposing parties to the transaction and any lenders, be proactive regarding diligence reviews and deliveries, and assist with pushing the transaction forward to closing by using checklists.

Kwame A. Benjamin is a partner in the Real Estate Department of Seyfarth Shaw LLP. His practice focuses on real estate matters. He represents clients in the leasing, acquisition, disposition, and development of commercial real estate, with a focus on retail and multi-family development, office, industrial and retail leasing, as well as secured lending transactions and general landlord/tenant matters. Mr. Benjamin also has experience representing both secured and unsecured creditors, and the defense of their rights, in bankruptcy proceedings.

Mr. Benjamin received a JD from Tulane Law School and a BS in accounting from Louisiana State University. He is an active member of ICSC and ULI.

Are We Headed Into "Seven Fat Years"?: What Real Estate Lawyers Can Expect for the Future

Dennis M. Horn

Partner and Co-Chair,
District of Columbia Practice Group
Holland & Knight LLP

ASPATORE

Introduction

What does the future hold for real estate lawyers? While the last three years have been pretty dismal, it appears that the real estate industry will emerge again along with the US economy. Real estate lawyers will be in the thick of it, although some of the work we now do will be commoditized and will pay less. Clients will continue to demand alternative fee arrangements and increasingly rapid communications with their lawyers. Lawyers who have a passion for sticks and bricks and the stomach to go through the booms and busts that define the real estate industry will have the opportunity to work with some of the brightest, most entrepreneurial clients in the country.

Understanding the Current Real Estate Market

Most of the United States is still under water in real estate, so the biggest trend we will see in coming years is the re-emergence of the market. Like the economy of biblical Egypt where seven fat years were followed by seven lean years, real estate has always been a cyclical industry. When interest rates are low and when the market anticipates inflation, commercial real estate is a good, stable investment. Since rents trend upward with inflation, real estate values also tend to rise. Similarly, since real estate is often heavily leveraged, the net operating income after debt service is typically stronger when a property is financed with low interest rate loans. Today, with oil prices through the roof, and food and commodity prices following, many believe that we are ripe for inflation. Interest rates are at historic lows and prices for commercial real estate have been reset at more sustainable levels after three years of recession. All of these factors combined will contribute to a strong real estate market in coming years.

As the recession wanes, demand for retail goods has increased. In fact, retail sales have increased by 7.9 percent from March 2010 to March 2011.[1] In addition, the tightening home mortgage market has meant that people who might have purchased a house or condo with easy credit are now moving into apartments. Because of both of these trends, retail outlets are expanding and, at least in the Washington, D.C. market, developers are building apartment projects again. For example, Disney announced in May

---

[1] *US Census Bureau News, US Dept. of Commerce, May 12, 2011 CB11-77.*

2011 that it was adding forty new retail locations around the country. The Peterson Companies announced in the same month that it is building a 350,000-square-foot, $100 million outlet mall adjacent to its National Harbor development outside of Washington, D.C.[2] These projects will generate construction and retail jobs.

The landscape is not completely positive. Lenders are still struggling to develop underwriting standards for new home mortgages that do not choke off the market. New federal laws will require stricter underwriting and more equity for new home purchases. Foreclosures are up in many parts of the country. The near demise of Fannie Mae and Freddie Mac means that the secondary mortgage market is in disarray. This will ultimately affect interest rates and loan terms, which will negatively affect the housing market. Banks are only slowly getting back into the business of real estate lending—especially for new development outside of the "hot" markets. Many willing workers are still unemployed or underemployed. Finally, gridlock in Congress undermines America's financial stability. However, in many parts of the United States, the real estate market is slowly recovering.

Interest rates, inflation, and consumer trends will influence the real estate market in the short to medium term. Demographics and jobs are more important for the long term. Both factors favor growth in the commercial real estate market. Between 2000 and 2010, the US population grew by 9.7 percent. The strongest population growth was in the South and West. Metro areas grew twice as fast as the national rate of growth. Houston, Atlanta, Dallas – Fort Worth, Washington, D.C., and Miami (in that order) were the fastest growing metro areas.[3]

The population of the United States is growing and more specifically, our young population is growing. This is largely due to immigration and the rising Hispanic population. Unlike places such as Japan, where the population is decreasing and getting older, the growing U.S. population will create and support growth in our economy. A growing population and a

---

[2] Ovetta Wiggins, "Outlet Center to Come to National Harbor," *The Washington Post*, May 23, 2011.
[3] *US Census Bureau, 2010 Census "Population Distribution and Change: 2000-2010,"* March 2011.

growing economy means that more housing, offices, and commercial real estate will be needed.

More jobs are also being created in the United States. *The Washington Post* reports that Indian outsourcing companies are moving back into the United States. One Indian-based outsourcing company, Aegis, expects to triple its US head count. According to the article, the "strategy is based on the old-fashioned idea of being close to your customers." Also, ""some U.S. companies don't want sensitive customer data transmitted abroad. Others are tired of poor service, accents and crackling phone lines."[4] Just as important, the wage disparities between US workers and foreign workers is shrinking fast. Hal Sirkin of the Boston Consulting Group is quoted as saying: "Pay for factory workers in China, for example, soared by 69% between 2005 and 2010…Sometime around 2015, manufacturers will be indifferent between locating in America or China for production for consumption in America."[5] At the same time, US manufacturing wages are declining in some industries. One example of this trend is in automobile manufacture. Volkswagen announced that they are opening a new plant in Tennessee with average wages of $27 per hour compared to Ford's average wages of $58 per hour.[6]

The tragic effects of the horrific tsunami in Japan will likely help commercial real estate in the United States. Because of the tragedy, manufacturing plants in Japan will not be able to supply parts for manufacturing plants in the United States and American manufacturers will reconsider locating their parts supply far away from their customers. *The Economist* article notes that, "complex supply chains turn out to be riskier than many firms realized. When oil prices soar, transport grows dearer. When an epidemic such as SARS hits Asia or when an earthquake hits Japan, supply chains are disrupted."[7]

---

[4] Paul Glader, "As Indian Companies Grow in the U.S., Outsourcing Comes Home," *The Washington Post* May 20, 2011.
[5] "Moving Back to America," *The Economist, May 12, 2011.*
[6] Mike Ramsey, "VW Chips Labor Costs in U.S.," *The Wall Street Journal,* May 23, 2011.
[7] *The Economist, supra*

In modern America, the concept of "just in time manufacturing" has been used for years. This means that manufacturers look for the most efficient plants anywhere in the world that can produce whatever they need "just in time" to use them on the finished product. For example, car companies in the United States have been using manufacturing plants in Mexico and Asia because they can produce the products cheaply and efficiently, and they can ship them to the United States in time to use them on the large frames of the cars. Since the tsunami occurred, the concept of "just in time manufacturing" has broken down. Toyota reports that it cannot meet the demand for spare parts or new cars in the United States this year because manufacturing plants affected by the tsunami are unable to produce the cars and parts. Toyota plants in the United States that depend on parts made in Japan will also be affected. When the economics of the global supply chain dictates that plants producing goods for the US market should be located in the United States, it means that more manufacturing jobs and warehousing will come back into the country. Even if the parts are produced abroad, higher shipping costs and uncertainty of supply mean that companies in the United States will have to stockpile the parts so they do not hold up their own production or so they can sell the latest fashions to their customers. As a result, they will need more US-based warehouses. Ultimately, more people in the United States will be employed. It is clear that these worldwide trends and costs of commodities will positively affect the need for real estate development in the United States. This is a good sign for real estate attorneys.

The Future for Real Estate Lawyers

The market for real estate lawyers follows the market for real estate. If you believe that the strongest real estate markets will follow population growth and jobs, it may make sense to locate in the South and West or in one of the fastest growing metro areas (Houston, Atlanta, Dallas – Fort Worth, Washington, D.C., or Miami). Wherever you are located, it is important to have a passion for what you do. Real estate law is fascinating. All entrepreneurs want to make money. Real estate entrepreneurs, and the brokers, lenders, analysts, and lawyers who work with them, also have the opportunity to change cities and communities for generations to come. As a group, real estate entrepreneurs are innovative and often fearless. As clients, they can be very demanding. Essentially, the lawyer's job is to anticipate the risks if possible, protect the client from those risks, and then get the deal closed.

Once a lawyer decides to practice real estate law, he or she has to decide between a commercial practice or a consumer practice. There is a huge division in our industry right now between commoditized real estate law and high value-added real estate law. The best example of commoditized, consumer-based real estate law is a house closing. Purchase contracts and mortgage forms are typically standardized. Most lawyers with any real estate background can maneuver through the forms, so there is a great deal of competition to supply the minimal legal services required. Consequently, legal fees for a house closing remain low. On the other hand, a lawyer can make a comfortable living with volume, especially if he or she also writes title insurance and handles the closing.

Lawyers are always needed when the documents are confusing or when one party is trying to impose unfair conditions. Since the consumer often will not recognize an unfair condition or a disguised business risk, the lawyer must identify the issues and provide advice to the client. Overall, this scenario has been largely eliminated in the home closing arena. In contrast, high value-added real estate legal work is created when a client has an incentive to hire the best lawyer possible because the transactional documents are not standard and allocate substantial risk and the cost of legal fees is small compared to the total cost of the asset.

As lawyers become more sophisticated, they develop procedures and forms that protect their clients. Typical commercial loan documents will protect the bank, sometimes with provisions that impose an unfair burden on the borrower. Some banks today have developed more even-handed forms. When the banks, the chain retailers, or large landlords who negotiate many documents, standardize their forms to include fair market provisions, the negotiations will go more quickly and the legal fees will be much less. When forms become standardized and are viewed as even handed, less legal input is required, and since many lawyers can do this type of legal work, it becomes commoditized.

Lawyers who want a high value-added practice, need to focus on specific areas so that they are providing a service that their clients value. Many successful lawyers reinvent themselves every five years. In the author's case, that has meant focusing on several areas over the years including elder housing law, single-family home development, office leasing, representing Amtrak in high speed rail development, acquisition, finance and development of retail facilities, conventional office facilities, warehouses, facilities leased to the federal government, and public/private partnerships. The lawyer has to develop the skills that his or her clients require. The lawyer also has to provide a value proposition to his or her clients. Often this means continually educating yourself in best practices and anticipating trends.

Organizing a Complex Real Estate Transaction

As a way to analyze best practices, let us examine a recent transaction that involved the acquisition of eleven office properties in eight states with equity and debt of more than $200 million.

The Team

The first step is to assemble a team of lawyers and consultants who can negotiate the contract, perform due diligence, set up the acquisition entities, arrange financing, and close the transaction. If the lawyer does not have the team in-house and if the lawyer does not have established relationships he or she can turn to, the American Bar Association membership list is a good place to look for local counsel. Efficiency is essential because the client is always interested in getting the best product at the best price. Sometimes when you have a big team working on a transaction, it is very challenging to get everybody on the same page at the same time. If this coordination doesn't occur, it can translate to a higher cost and delays for the client.

Communication is the most important strategy when working with a large team. Lawyers should know what they want to accomplish from the very beginning and should get the principal players involved as quickly as possible in order to determine how the process will progress. It is always important to obtain effective written documents and checklists that assign responsibilities and monitor each team member to make sure everyone understands what they are supposed to be doing and when each task should be completed. Included as Appendix P is a checklist for a "prototype" transaction. The team leader's first priority is to manage the process so that the transaction crosses the finish line on time and on budget. The team leader's second priority is to set realistic budget and time expectations—both for the lawyers and for the client. Clients never like to be surprised by legal fees or missed deadlines.

The Contract

The seller would like to see a two-page contract that identifies the property and the price and requires the purchaser to buy the property on a set date in "as is" condition with a large deposit to ensure closing. The purchaser would like a contract in which the seller represents what the purchaser is buying and covenants to maintain the property prior to closing, sets conditions of closing, allows a property inspection before the purchaser is committed, and holds the seller liable for misrepresentations. Since the seller is often a single-purpose entity that will distribute its cash to its members after closing, the contract also needs to provide security for the seller's representations, either in the form of a solvent guarantor or in the form of cash or a letter of credit. The lawyer's art is to negotiate a contract that addresses all these conflicting objectives.

Due Diligence

The seller will provide access to the property and copies of the leases, service contracts, environmental reports, cost and income reports, plans and specifications, permits, zoning reports, and other relevant information to allow the purchaser to understand the property that it is buying. The lawyer's task is to update the title, identify the title exceptions that will be permitted, review the environmental reports and zoning and permitting issues, and answer whatever questions the client may have about the property. The client will typically also engage a property inspector and an appraiser, and will conduct new environmental studies of the property. Even when the purchase contract includes reasonable representations, a buyer and the buyer's lawyer should always assume that "buyer beware" applies and should kick the tires thoroughly before committing to purchase a property.

Financing

Financing comes in a least two parts: equity and debt. In a large acquisition like this one, debt will typically be between 65 percent and 75 percent of value. If it is conventional debt, the loan documents will start with the lender's standard form and will then be negotiated to conform to the commitment letter the client obtained from the lender. If it is securitized debt, the forms will be fairly standard so that they meet both underwriting and rating agency criteria. In either case, the lawyer must make sure that the business deal is reflected in the loan documents. Often equity is provided by a private fund or real estate investment trust. In the case of a private fund, the equity has been raised pursuant to a private placement memorandum and is available for any deal that meets the criteria set forth in the offering memorandum. Alternatively, a developer might form a joint venture with an equity source to acquire the property. In that case, the business deal, which includes control provisions, risk allocation, and profit distribution, will be set forth in a joint venture agreement or a limited liability operating agreement. The lender will often require that the buyer be a newly formed single-purpose entity and will require opinion letters that may include a non-consolidation opinion as well as "due formation" and authority opinions.

Closing

The transaction comes together in the closing. The purchaser's lawyer prepares the conveyance documents, the lease assignments, the subordination and non-disturbance agreements, and oversees the execution of the loan documents and the conveyance documents. The lawyer will also issue his or her opinion letters to the lender and coordinate title insurance on the acquisition both for the purchaser and for the lender.

Challenges for Real Estate Lawyers in Today's Market

In the practice of real estate law, it is inevitable that lawyers will engage with challenging clients. The most challenging clients are those who do not really know what they want and keep changing their minds as the process goes along. In ongoing development projects where clients have land they want to build on, they often assess the market differently as time goes on. They might begin wanting to build an apartment complex, but a year later decide they really want to build a condominium complex. However, since the initial contracts were written for the apartments, the lawyers are often forced to make changes in the middle of the deal in order to accommodate the new developments. The biggest challenge for the lawyer is to anticipate these types of potential problems and try to build enough flexibility into the contract so that when they do arise, the problems can be fixed relatively easily.

Client Expectations

A smart entrepreneurial client expects to make mistakes because he or she knows that success comes from taking risks—and taking risks means that you do not always win. People who are not willing to make mistakes never realize their dreams. On the other hand, modern society is very litigious and a careless entrepreneur can lose much more than he bargained for. These entrepreneurial clients hire lawyers to figure out where the risks are and how to minimize the consequences of making those mistakes. For example, the client may avoid personally guaranteeing loans so that if the restaurant or other venture fails, the client will lose some cash, but will keep his or her larger assets. It is up to the lawyer to make sure the client understands the risks and is protected from risks he or she is not prepared to take.

Lawyers also often fail to anticipate how long it takes for third parties, such as appraisers, surveyors, and environmentalists to complete their tasks. It is also common for lawyers to underestimate legal fees. Clients want predictable legal fees and deadlines that are met. Once again, they hate surprises. Unfortunately, the legal costs often depend on third parties. A smart, reasonable lawyer on the other side can make a deal quickly. A difficult or badly informed lawyer can make the deal a nightmare. Similarly, a recalcitrant title company or appraiser can hold up a closing. One way or the other, lawyers are going to have to deal with unpredictable fees and tight deadlines. Clients want certainty and clients ultimately get what they want.

Conclusion

It seems that we are about to enter the "fat years" in the real estate cycle. We are not there yet, but the demographics are with us and the business cycles appear to be coming into line. America is experiencing a slow recovery, and as the economy becomes revitalized, so will the real estate market. For the past three years, buyers expected real estate prices to fall and sellers expected prices to rise. Lenders were not lending and no one was transacting business. The fact that many commercial assets have been re-priced to the current market is great for lawyers. Lawyers will make money as long as clients are making deals. Clients will make deals as long as property is priced to the market and loans are available. In the long term, real estate law is a great field for those with a passion for deal-making and for seeing tangible results in brick and mortar from their legal work.

Key Takeaways

- Be passionate about what you do. With passion you can feel rewarded by your legal career and know that you are truly contributing to the success of your clients and perhaps to building your community.
- Communicate effectively with your client and with other members of your legal team so everyone knows their jobs and their deadlines.
- Avoid surprising your client by anticipating how much various services will cost and how long tasks, such as document negotiation, appraisals, and inspections, will take.
- Clients expect value from their lawyers. The days are behind us when clients were prepared to pay whatever their lawyers billed. Be prepared to deliver a product for a price.
- Be prepared to reinvent yourself every five years by anticipating new trends so that you will have the expertise that the clients will require.

Dennis M. Horn is a partner in Holland & Knight's Washington, D.C. office and co-chair of the District of Columbia Practice Group. Mr. Horn is a transactional attorney practicing primarily in the real property area, emphasizing acquisition and development, commercial leasing (including space leases, GSA leases, and ground leases), public-private partnerships, joint ventures, loans, and equity investments and workouts. He also practices in various aspects of government operations.

Mr. Horn has lectured and written extensively about various aspects of commercial real estate development. He represented Amtrak in the real estate development and financing of the $1.1 billion high-speed rail project and the subsequent financing of various rail yards. He also led a team of lawyers representing a multinational developer in the acquisition, development, and leasing of various mixed-use and retail real estate projects aggregating more than 800,000 square feet in Georgetown and in the West End of Washington, D.C. Mr. Horn also led another team of lawyers and other professionals representing a private real estate fund in the acquisition, development, and dispositions of more than $1.5 billion of real estate nationwide leased to the federal government. He has also worked on public/private partnerships to provide university student housing, new public facilities, retail facilities, and both market rate and affordable housing.

Acknowledgment: *I would like to thank Shundra Frasier, Paula Burk, and Elizabeth A. Blake, all of Holland & Knight LLP, for their help in researching, editing, and producing this chapter.*

APPENDICES

Appendix A: Critical Dates Schedule — 110

Appendix B: Commercial Real Estate Contract Form — 113

Appendix C: Allonge Blank Form — 126

Appendix D: Bill of Sale Form — 127

Appendix E: Assignment of Mortgage and Other Loan Documents — 130

Appendix F: Warranty Deed Form — 134

Appendix G: Seller Affidavit Form — 137

Appendix H: Due Diligence Disposition Checklist — 140

Appendix I: General Checklist for Construction — 150

Appendix J: Owner's Checklist for Responding to New York Mechanics' Liens — 155

Appendix K: Loan Closing Checklist — 161

Appendix L: Statutory Acknowledgment Forms — 169

Appendix M: Early Access Agreement Form — 171

Appendix N: Due Diligence Checklist — 175

Appendix O: Real Property Purchase Agreement — 181

Appendix P: Sample Closing Checklist — 203

APPENDIX A

CRITICAL DATES SCHEDULE

(Matter #_____)

CONTRACT OF SALE AND PURCHASE
by and among

_____
("Purchaser")

and

_____
("Seller")

Property:_____

Purchase Price: $_____

Due Date/ Time	Action Required	Section	Status
	Effective Date		
	Purchaser to deposit $_____ Initial Earnest Money with Escrow Agent		
	Seller to deliver to Purchaser surveys, title commitments, title policies, reports, plans, etc. in its possession relating to Property		
	Purchaser to order Title Commitment and provide copy to Seller's counsel		
	Purchaser may obtain Survey		

Due Date/ Time	Action Required	Section	Status
	Purchaser to review title and survey matters and provide written notice to Seller of Title Defects		
	Seller shall notify Purchaser whether it elects to cure or remove any Title Defects ("Purchaser's Notice")		
	If elected, Purchaser to remove or cure Title Defects ("Cure Period")		
	Purchaser to give Seller notice of termination of Contract or elect in writing to waive any Title Defect		
	Inspection Period Expires		
	Purchaser to notify Seller if Purchaser will be assuming any of the Service Contracts		
	Purchaser to deposit $_____ ("Second Earnest Money Deposit") with Escrow Agent if Purchaser does not terminate Contract.		
	Closing Date		

PROPER NOTICE
All notices, demands, or other communications of any type (herein collectively referred to as "Notices") given by the Seller to the Purchaser, or by the Purchaser to the Seller, whether required by this Contract or in any way related to the transaction contracted for herein, shall be void and of no effect unless given in accordance with the provisions of this Article 15.1. All notices shall be in writing and delivered to the person to whom the Notice is directed, either: (i) in person; (ii) by United States Mail, certified with return receipt requested; (iii) delivered by Federal Express or other comparable overnight courier which obtains a receipt to confirm delivery; or (iv) sent by telex or telecopy with confirmed receipt. Notices delivered by mail shall be deemed given three (3) days after deposited in a post office or other depository under the care or custody of the United States Postal Service, enclosed in a wrapper, addressed properly, with proper postage affixed. All notices shall be addressed as follows:

FOR PURCHASER: **FOR SELLER:**

With a copy to: With a copy to:

ESCROW AGENT:

Courtesy of Shari B. Olefson, Fowler White Boggs PA

APPENDIX B

COMMERCIAL REAL ESTATE CONTRACT FORM

1. PURCHASE AND SALE: _____ ("Buyer")

agrees to buy and _____ ("Seller")

agrees to sell the property described as: Street Address: _____
_____

Legal Description: _____

and the following Personal Property: _____
_____

(all collectively referred to as the "Property") on the terms and conditions set forth below. **The "Effective Date" of this Contract is the date on which the last of the Parties signs the latest offer. Time is of the essence in this Contract.** Time periods of 5 days or less will be computed without including Saturday, Sunday, or national legal holidays and any time period ending on a Saturday, Sunday or national legal holiday will be extended until 5:00 p.m. of the next business day.

2. **PURCHASE PRICE:** $_____

    a. Deposit held in escrow by _____
                                                                        $_____

    b. Additional deposit to be made within _____ days
        from Effective Date $_____

    c. Total mortgages (as referenced in Paragraph 3)
                                                                        $_____

d. Other: _____

$ _____

e. Balance to close, subject to adjustments and prorations, to be made with cash, locally drawn certified or cashier's check or wire transfer.

$ _____

3. **THIRD PARTY FINANCING:** Within _____ days from Effective Date ("Application Period"), Buyer will, at Buyer's expense, apply for third party financing in the amount of $ _____ or _____% of the purchase price to be amortized over a period of _____ years and due in no less than _____ years and with a fixed interest rate not to exceed _____% per year or variable interest rate not to exceed _____ % at origination with a lifetime cap not to exceed _____ % from initial rate, with additional terms as follows:

_____

Buyer will pay for the mortgagee title insurance policy and for all loan expenses. Buyer will timely provide any and all credit, employment, financial and other information reasonably required by any lender. Buyer will notify Seller immediately upon obtaining financing or being rejected by a lender. If Buyer, after diligent effort, fails to obtain a written commitment within _____ days from Effective Date ("Financing Period"), Buyer may cancel the Contract by giving prompt notice to Seller and Buyer's deposit(s) will be returned to Buyer in accordance with Paragraph 9.

Buyer (_____) (_____) and Seller (_____) (_____) acknowledge receipt of a copy of this page, which is page 1 of 5 Pages.

4. **TITLE:** Seller has the legal capacity to and will convey marketable title to the Property by

☐ statutory warranty deed
☐ other _____, free of liens, easements and encumbrances of record or known to Seller, but subject to property taxes for the year of closing; covenants, restrictions and

public utility easements of record; and (list any other matters to which title will be subject)_____
_____;
provided there exists at closing no violation of the foregoing and none of them prevents **Buyer's** intended use of the Property as
_____.

a. **Evidence of Title: Title Agent** will, at ____ Sellers/____ Buyer's expense and within ____ days from Effective Date _____ prior to Closing Date ____ from date Buyer meets or waives financing contingency in Paragraph 3, deliver to Buyer (check one)

____ a title insurance commitment by a Florida licensed title insurer and, upon Buyer recording the deed, an owner's policy in the amount of the purchase price for fee simple title subject only to exceptions stated above.

____ an abstract of title, prepared or brought current by an existing abstract firm or certified as correct by an existing firm. However, if such an abstract is not available to Seller, then a prior owner's title policy acceptable to the proposed insurer as a base for re-issuance of coverage is acceptable. The prior policy will include copies of all policy exceptions and an update in a format acceptable to Buyer from the policy effective date and certified to Buyer or Buyer's closing agent together with copies of all documents recited in the prior policy and in the update.

b. **Title Examination:** Buyer will, within 15 days from receipt of the evidence of title deliver written notice to Seller of title defects. Title will be deemed acceptable to Buyer if (1) Buyer fails to deliver proper notice of defects or (2) Buyer delivers proper written notice and Seller cures the defects within ____ days from receipt of the notice ("Curative Period"). If the defects are cured within the Curative Period, closing will occur within 10 days from receipt by Buyer of notice of such curing. Seller may elect not to cure defects if Seller reasonably believes any defect cannot be cured within the Curative Period. If the defects are not cured within the Curative Period, Buyer will have 10 days from receipt of notice of Seller's inability to cure the defects to elect whether to terminate this Contract or accept title subject to existing defects and close the transaction without reduction in purchase price. The party who pays for the evidence of title will also pay related title service fees including title and abstract charges and title examination.

   c. **Survey:** (check applicable provisions below)

_____ Seller will, within _____ days from Effective Date, deliver to Buyer copies of prior surveys, plans, specifications, and engineering documents, if any, and the following documents relevant to this transaction:_____, prepared for Seller or in Seller's possession, which show all currently existing structures.

_____ Buyer will, at ____ Seller's ____ Buyer's expense and within the time period allowed to deliver and examine title evidence, obtain a current certified survey of the Property from a registered surveyor. If the survey reveals encroachments on the Property or that the improvements encroach on the lands of another, ____ Buyer will accept the Property with existing encroachments ____ such encroachments will constitute a title defect to be cured within the Curative Period.

   d. **Ingress and Egress:** Seller warrants that the Property presently has ingress and egress.

   e. **Possession:** Seller will deliver possession and keys for all locks and alarms to Buyer at closing.

5. **CLOSING DATE AND PROCEDURE:** This transaction will be closed in _____ County, Florida on or before the _____ or within _____ days from Effective Date ("Closing Date"), unless otherwise extended herein. ____ Seller/____ Buyer will designate the closing agent. Buyer and Seller will, within _____ days from Effective Date, deliver to Escrow Agent signed instructions which provide for closing procedure. If an institutional lender is providing purchase funds, lender requirements as

to place, time of day and closing procedures will control over any contrary provisions in this Contract.

a. **Costs:** Buyer will pay taxes and recording fees on notes, mortgages and financing statements and recording fees for the deed. Seller will pay taxes on the deed and recording fees for documents needed to cure title defects. If Seller is obligated to discharge any encumbrance at or prior to closing and fails to do so, Buyer may use purchase proceeds to satisfy the encumbrances.

b. **Documents:** Seller will provide the deed, bill of sale, mechanic's lien affidavit, assignments of leases, updated rent roll, tenant and Lender estoppel letters, assignments of permits and licenses, corrective instruments and letters notifying tenants of the change in ownership/rental agent. If any tenant refuses to execute an estoppel letter, Seller will certify that information regarding the tenant's lease is correct. If Seller is a corporation, Seller will deliver a resolution of its Board of Directors authorizing the sale and delivery of the deed and certification by the corporate Secretary certifying the resolution and setting forth facts showing the conveyance conforms to the requirements of local law. Seller will transfer security deposits to Buyer. Buyer will provide the closing statement, mortgages and notes, security agreements and financing statements.

c. **Taxes, Assessments, and Prorations:** The following items will be made current and prorated _____ as of Closing Date_____ as of _____ : real estate taxes, bond and assessment payments assumed by Buyer, interest, rents, association dues, insurance premiums acceptable to Buyer, operational expenses and _____

If the amount of taxes and assessments for the current year cannot be ascertained, rates for the previous year will be used with due allowance being made for improvements and exemptions. Seller is aware of the following assessments affecting or potentially affecting the Property: _____.

Buyer will be responsible for all assessments of any kind which become due and owing on or after Effective Date, unless the improvement is substantially completed as of Closing Date, in which case Seller will be obligated to pay the entire assessment.

    d. **FIRPTA Tax Withholding:** The Foreign Investment in Real Property Act ("FIRPTA") requires Buyer to withhold at closing a portion of the purchase proceeds for remission to the Internal Revenue Service ("I.R.S.") if Seller is a "foreign person" as defined by the Internal Revenue Code. The parties agree to comply with the provisions of FIRPTA and to provide, at or prior to closing, appropriate documentation to establish any applicable exemption from the withholding requirement. If withholding is required and Buyer does not have cash sufficient at closing to meet the withholding requirement, Seller will provide the necessary funds and Buyer will provide proof to Seller that such funds were properly remitted to the I.R.S.

6. **ESCROW and TITLE:** Buyer and Seller authorize _____
Telephone: _____ Facsimile: _____
Address: _____to act as "Escrow Agent" and "Title Agent" to receive funds and other items and, subject to clearance, disburse them in accordance with the terms of this Contract. Escrow Agent will deposit all funds received in _____ a non-interest bearing escrow account _____ an interest bearing escrow account with interest accruing to _____ with interest disbursed (check one) __ at closing __ at _____ intervals. If Escrow Agent receives conflicting demands or has a good faith doubt as to Escrow Agent's duties or liabilities under this Contract, he/she may (a) hold the subject matter of the escrow until the parties mutually agree to its disbursement or until issuance of a court order or decision of arbitrator determining the parties' rights regarding the escrow or (b) deposit the subject matter of the escrow with the clerk of the circuit court having jurisdiction over the dispute. Upon notifying the parties of such action, Escrow Agent will be released from all liability except for the duty to account for items previously delivered out of escrow. If a licensed real estate broker, Escrow Agent will comply with applicable

provisions of Chapter 475, Florida Statutes. In any suit or arbitration in which Escrow Agent is made a party because of acting as agent hereunder or interpleads the subject matter of the escrow, Escrow Agent will recover reasonable attorneys' fees and costs at all levels, with such fees and costs to be paid from the escrowed funds or equivalent and charged and awarded as court or other costs in favor of the prevailing party. The parties agree that Escrow Agent will not be liable to any person for misdelivery to Buyer or Seller of escrowed items, unless the misdelivery is due to Escrow Agent's willful breach of this Contract or gross negligence.

7. **PROPERTY CONDITION:** Seller will deliver the Property to Buyer at the time agreed in its present "as is" condition, ordinary wear and tear accepted, and will maintain the landscaping and grounds in a comparable condition. Seller makes no warranties other than marketability of title. By accepting the Property "as is," Buyer waives all claims against Seller for any defects in the property.

(Check (a) or (b))

a. ____**As Is:** Buyer has inspected the Property or waives any right to inspect and accepts the Property in its "as is" condition.

b. ____**Due Diligence Period:** Buyer will, at Buyer's expense and within ____ days from Effective Date ("Due Diligence Period"), determine whether the Property is suitable, in Buyer's sole and absolute discretion, for Buyer's intended use and development of the Property as specified in Paragraph 4. During the Due Diligence Period, Buyer may conduct any tests, analyses, surveys and investigations ("Inspections") which Buyer deems necessary to determine to Buyer's satisfaction the Property's engineering, architectural, environmental properties; zoning and zoning restrictions; flood zone designation and restrictions; subdivision regulations; soil and grade; availability of access to public roads, water, and other utilities; consistency with local, state and regional growth management and comprehensive land use plans; availability of permits, government approvals and licenses; compliance with American with Disabilities Act; absence of asbestos, soil and ground water contamination; and other inspections that Buyer deems appropriate to determine the suitability of the Property for Buyer's intended use and development. Buyer shall deliver written notice to Seller prior to the expiration of the Due Diligence Period of Buyer's determination of whether or not the Property is acceptable. Buyer's failure to comply with this notice requirement shall constitute acceptance of the Property in its present "as is" condition. Seller grants to Buyer, its agents, contractors and assigns, the right to enter the Property at any time during the Due Diligence Period for the purpose of conducting Inspections; provided, however, that Buyer, its agents, contractors and assigns enter the Property and conduct Inspections at their own risk. Buyer shall indemnify and hold Seller harmless from losses, damages, costs, claims and expenses of any nature, including attorneys' fees at all levels, and from liability to any person, arising from the conduct of any and all inspections or any work authorized by Buyer. Buyer will not engage in any activity that could result in a mechanic's lien being filed against the Property without Seller's prior written consent. In the event this transaction does not close, (1) Buyer shall repair all damages to the Property resulting from the Inspections and return the Property to the condition it was in prior to conduct of the inspections, and (2) Buyer shall, at Buyer's expense, release to Seller all reports and other work generated as a result of the Inspections. Should Buyer deliver timely notice that the Property is not acceptable, Seller agrees that Buyer's deposit shall be immediately returned to Buyer and the Contract terminated.

c. **Walk-through Inspection: Buyer** may, on the day prior to closing or any other time mutually agreeable to the parties, conduct a final "walk-through" inspection of the Property to determine compliance with this paragraph and to ensure that all Property is on the premises.

d. **Disclosures:**

1. **Radon Gas**: Radon is a naturally occurring radioactive gas that, when it has accumulated in a building in sufficient

quantities, may present health risks to persons who are exposed to it over time. Levels of radon that exceed federal and state guidelines have been found in buildings in Florida. Additional information regarding radon and radon testing may be obtained from your county public health unit.

2. **Energy Efficiency:** Buyer may have determined the energy efficiency rating of the building, if any is located on the Real Property.

8. **OPERATION OF PROPERTY** DURING CONTRACT PERIOD: Seller will continue to operate the Property and any business conducted on the Property in the manner operated prior to Contract and will take no action that would adversely impact the Property, tenants, lenders or business, if any. Any changes, such as renting vacant space, that materially affects the Property or Buyer's intended use of the Property will be permitted ____ only with Buyer's consent ____ without Buyer's consent.

9. **RETURN OF DEPOSIT:** Unless otherwise specified in the Contract, in the event any condition of this Contract is not met and Buyer has timely given any required notice regarding the condition having not been met, Buyer's deposit will be returned in accordance with applicable Florida laws and regulations.

10. **DEFAULT:**

    a. In the event the sale is not closed due to any default or failure on the part of Seller other than failure to make the title marketable after diligent effort, Buyer may either (1) receive a refund of Buyer's deposit(s) or (2) seek specific performance. If Buyer elects a deposit refund, Seller will be liable to Broker for the full amount of the brokerage fee.

    b. In the event the sale is not closed due to any default or failure on the part of Buyer, Seller may either (1) retain all deposit(s) paid or agreed to be paid by Buyer as agreed upon liquidated damages, consideration for the execution of this Contract, and in full settlement of any claims, upon which this Contract will terminate or (2) seek specific performance. If Seller retains the deposit, Seller will pay the Listing and Cooperating Brokers named in Paragraph 12 fifty percent of all forfeited deposits retained by Seller (to be split equally among the Brokers) up to the full amount of the brokerage fee.

11. **ATTORNEY'S FEES AND COSTS**: In any claim or controversy arising out of or relating to this Contract, the prevailing party, which for purposes of this provision will include Buyer, Seller and Broker, will be awarded reasonable attorneys' fees, costs and expenses.

12. **BROKERS**: Neither Buyer nor Seller has utilized the services of, or for any other reason owes compensation to, a licensed real estate Broker other than:

   a. **Listing Broker:** _____,
   who is ___ an agent of _____
   _____ a transaction broker ____ a nonrepresentative and who will be compensated by __Seller __ Buyer ___both parties pursuant to __ a listing agreement
   ___ other (specify)

   _____
   _____

   b. **Cooperating Broker:** _____
   who is ___ an agent of _____
   ___ a transaction broker ___ a nonrepresentative and who will be compensated by __Seller ___ Buyer ___ both parties pursuant to___ an MLS or other offer of compensation to a cooperating broker ___ other (specify)

   _____
   _____

(collectively referred to as "Broker") in connection with any act relating to the Property, including but not limited to inquiries, introductions, consultations and negotiations resulting in this transaction. Seller and

Buyer agree to indemnify and hold Broker harmless from and against losses, damages, costs and expenses of any kind, including reasonable attorneys' fees at all levels, and from liability to any person, arising from (1) compensation claimed which is inconsistent with the representation in this Paragraph, (2) enforcement action to collect a brokerage fee pursuant to Paragraph 10, (3) any duty accepted by Broker at the request of Buyer or Seller, which duty is beyond the scope of services regulated by Chapter 475, F.S., as amended, or (4) recommendations of or services provided and expenses incurred by any third party whom Broker refers, recommends or retains for or on behalf of Buyer or Seller.

13. **ASSIGNABILITY; PERSONS BOUND**: This Contract may be assigned to a related entity, and otherwise ____ is not assignable ____ is assignable. The terms "Buyer," "Seller" and "Broker" may be singular or plural. This Contract is binding upon Buyer, Seller and their heirs, personal representatives, successors and assigns (if assignment is permitted).

14. **OPTIONAL CLAUSES:** (Check if any of the following clauses are applicable and are attached as an addendum to this Contract):

    ☐ Arbitration   ☐ Seller Warranty
    ☐ Existing Mortgage   ☐ Section 1031 Exchange
    ☐ Seller Financing   ☐ Seller Representations
    ☐ Coastal Construction Control Line   ☐ Other _____
    ☐ Property Inspection and Repair   ☐ Other _____
    ☐ Flood Area Hazard Zone   ☐ Other _____

15. **MISCELLANEOUS:** The terms of this Contract constitute the entire agreement between **Buyer** and **Seller**. Modifications of this Contract will not be binding unless in writing, signed and delivered by the party to be bound. Signatures, initials, documents referenced in this Contract, counterparts and written modifications communicated electronically or on paper will be acceptable for all purposes, including delivery, and will be binding. Handwritten or typewritten terms inserted in or attached to this Contract prevail over preprinted terms. If any provision of this Contract is or becomes invalid or unenforceable, all

remaining provisions will continue to be fully effective. This Contract will be construed under Florida law and will not be recorded in any public records. Delivery of any written notice to any party's agent will be deemed delivery to that party.

THIS IS INTENDED TO BE A LEGALLY BINDING CONTRACT. IF NOT FULLY UNDERSTOOD, SEEK THE ADVICE OF AN ATTORNEY PRIOR TO SIGNING. BROKER ADVISES BUYER AND SELLER TO VERIFY ALL FACTS AND REPRESENTATIONS THAT ARE IMPORTANT TO THEM AND TO CONSULT AN APPROPRIATE PROFESSIONAL FOR LEGAL ADVICE (FOR EXAMPLE, INTERPRETING CONTRACTS, DETERMINING THE EFFECT OF LAWS ON THE PROPERTY AND TRANSACTION, STATUS OF TITLE, FOREIGN INVESTOR REPORTING REQUIREMENTS, ETC.) AND FOR TAX, PROPERTY CONDITION, ENVIRONMENTAL AND OTHER SPECIALIZED ADVICE. BUYER ACKNOWLEDGES THAT BROKER DOES NOT OCCUPY THE PROPERTY AND THAT ALL REPRESENTATIONS (ORAL, WRITTEN OR OTHERWISE) BY BROKER ARE BASED ON SELLER REPRESENTATIONS OR PUBLIC RECORDS UNLESS BROKER INDICATES PERSONAL VERIFICATION OF THE REPRESENTATION. BUYER AGREES TO RELY SOLELY ON SELLER, PROFESSIONAL INSPECTORS AND GOVERNMENTAL AGENCIES FOR VERIFICATION OF THE PROPERTY CONDITION, SQUARE FOOTAGE AND FACTS THAT MATERIALLY AFFECT PROPERTY VALUE.

DEPOSIT RECEIPT: Deposit of $ _____ by _____ check ___ other _____ received on _____, _____ by _____
Signature of Escrow Agent

OFFER: Buyer offers to purchase the Property on the above terms and conditions. Unless acceptance is signed by Seller and a signed copy delivered to Buyer or Buyer's agent no later than _____ a.m. ___ p.m. on _____, _____, Buyer may revoke this offer and receive a refund of all deposits.

Date: _____ BUYER: _____ Tax ID No: _____

        Title: _____ Telephone: _____ Facsimile: _____
        Address: _____

Date: _____ BUYER: _____ Tax ID No: _____

        Title: _____ Telephone: _____ Facsimile: _____
        Address: _____

ACCEPTANCE: Seller accepts Buyer's offer and agrees to sell the Property on the above terms and conditions (____ subject to the attached counter offer).

Date: _____ SELLER: _____ Tax ID No: _____

        Title: _____ Telephone: _____ Facsimile: _____
        Address: _____

Date: _____ SELLER: _____ Tax ID No: _____

        Title: _____ Telephone: _____ Facsimile: _____
        Address: _____

Courtesy of Shari B. Olefson, Fowler White Boggs PA

APPENDIX C

ALLONGE BLANK FORM

This Allonge is effective as of _____ and is attached to and made a part of the following Promissory Note:

That certain Promissory Note dated _____, in the original principal amount of _____ AND 0/100 DOLLARS ($_____.00) made by _____, a _____ in favor of _____.

PAY TO THE ORDER OF _____, WITHOUT RECOURSE, REPRESENTATION OR WARRANTY, EXPRESS OR IMPLIED.

By:_____
Name:_____, its Attorney-in-Fact

Courtesy of Shari B. Olefson, Fowler White Boggs PA

APPENDIX D

BILL OF SALE FORM

BILL OF SALE, ABSOLUTE

KNOW ALL MEN BY THESE PRESENTS:

That _____, a _____, whose post office address is _____, party of the first part, for and in consideration of the sum of _____ DOLLARS ($_____) lawful money of the United States, to be paid by _____, a _____, party of the second part, the receipt whereof is hereby acknowledged, has granted, bargained, sold, transferred, and delivered, and by these presents do grant, bargain, sell, transfer and deliver unto the party of the second part, their executors, administrators and assigns, the following goods and chattels located on the property at _____ and further described on <u>Exhibit A</u>, attached hereto and made a part hereof:

INSERT LIST OF ITEMS

To Have and To Hold the same unto the said party of the second part, their executors, administrators and assigns forever.

And they do for themselves and their heirs, executors and administrators, covenant to and with the party of the second part, their executors administrators and assigns that they are the lawful owners of the said goods and chattels; that they are free from all encumbrances; that they have good right to sell the same aforesaid, and that they will warrant and defend the sale of the said property, goods and chattels hereby made, unto the said party of the second part, their executors, administrators and assigns against the lawful claims and demands of all persons whomsoever.

In Witness Whereof, the party of the first part has hereunto set their hands and seals this _____ day of _____, 20_____.

Signed, sealed and delivered in the presence of:

_____
Printed Name:_____

_____
Printed Name:_____

STATE OF FLORIDA

COUNTY OF _____

The foregoing instrument was acknowledged before me this _____ day of _____, 20___, by _____, as _____ of _____, a _____, who is personally known to me or who has produced _____ as identification.

My Commission Expires: _____
                                                    Notary Public

EXHIBIT A

LEGAL DESCRIPTION

Courtesy of Shari B. Olefson, Fowler White Boggs PA

APPENDIX E

ASSIGNMENT OF MORTGAGE
AND OTHER LOAN DOCUMENTS

Prepared by & return to:
_____, Esq.
_____, P.A.
_____
_____

KNOW ALL MEN BY THESE PRESENTS,

THAT _____ (**"Assignor"**), residing or located at _____, for and in consideration of the sum of $1.00 dollar and other good and valuable consideration, the receipt of which is hereby acknowledged, does hereby grant, bargain, sell, assign, transfer and set over unto _____, (**"Assignee"**), the mortgage and other loan documents described on **EXHIBIT A** attached hereto and made a part hereof, together with all other loan documents executed in connection therewith, all of which are hereby assigned and endorsed to the Assignee this date, and all money due to and become due thereon, WITHOUT RECOURSE. The Assignee is not acting as nominee of the mortgagor and the mortgage continues to secure a bona fide obligation.

TO HAVE AND TO HOLD the same unto the Assignee and to the successors, legal representatives and assigns of the Assignee forever, and Assignor hereby constitutes and appoints said Assignee its attorney irrevocable to collect and receive said debt, and to foreclose, enforce, and satisfy said lien the same as it might or could have done were these presents not executed, but at the cost and expense of the Assignee.

This assignment is made without recourse, representation or warranty, express or implied, by the Federal Deposit Insurance Corporation, in its capacity as receiver.

By:_____
Name:_____, its
Attorney-in-Fact[1]

STATE OF _____)
COUNTY OF _____)

The foregoing instrument was acknowledged before me this ___ day of _____, _____, by _____, in its capacity as receiver for _____, on behalf of the bank. He/She [ ] is personally known to me OR [ ] produced a _____ state drivers license as identification.

_____
Name:_____
Notary Public, State of _____
My Commission Expires:_____
Commission Number:_____
My Commission Expires:_____
[Notary Seal]

---

[1] See Exhibit B attached hereto for copy of Limited Power of Attorney.

EXHIBIT A

1. Loan documents to be assigned:

    a. Mortgage, Security Agreement and Assignment of Rents, dated _____, recorded _____, in Official Records Book _____, Page ____, as modified by that certain Modification of Mortgage dated _____, recorded _____, in Official Records Book _____, Page ____, all of the Public Records of _____ County.
    b. Real Estate Assignment of Rents and Leases, dated _____, and recorded in Official Records Book _____, Page ____, Public Records of _____ County.
    c. Promissory Note, dated _____, in the principal amount of _____ Dollars and No Cents ($_____.00).
    d. Change in Terms Agreement dated _____.
    e. Unconditional Guarantee, dated _____, from _____, individually.
    f. Related UCC financing statement described as follows:

        i. UCC-1 filed in Official Records Book _____, Page _____ of the Public Records of _____ County.

EXHIBIT B
(Power of Attorney)

Courtesy of Shari B. Olefson, Fowler White Boggs PA

APPENDIX F

WARRANTY DEED FORM

THIS INSTRUMENT PREPARED BY AND RETURN TO:

Property Appraisers Parcel Identification (Folio) Number:

_____SPACE ABOVE THIS LINE FOR RECORDING DATA_____

THIS WARRANTY DEED, made the _____ day of _____,
20____, by _____,
herein called the Grantor, to _____,
whose post office address is _____,
hereinafter called the Grantees:

(Wherever used herein the terms "grantor" and "grantee" include all the parties to this instrument and the heirs, legal representatives and assigns of individuals, and the successors and assigns of corporations)

W I T N E S S E T H: That the grantor, for and in consideration of the sum of TEN AND 00/100'S ($10.00) Dollars and other valuable considerations, receipt whereof is hereby acknowledged, hereby grants, bargains, sells, aliens, remises, releases, conveys and confirms unto the grantee all that certain land situate in _____ County, State of Florida, viz.:

(Insert Legal Description)

Subject to easements, restrictions and reservations of record and to taxes for the year 2003 and thereafter.

TOGETHER, with all the tenements, hereditaments and appurtenances thereto belonging or in anywise appertaining.

TO HAVE AND TO HOLD, the same in fee simple forever.

AND, the grantor hereby covenants with said grantees that the grantor is lawfully seized of said land in fee simple; that the grantor has good right and lawful authority to sell and convey said land, and hereby warrants the title to said land and will defend the same against the lawful claims of all persons whomsoever; and that said land is free of all encumbrances, except taxes accruing subsequent to December 31, 20_____.

IN WITNESS WHEREOF, the said grantor has signed and sealed these presents the day and year first above written.

Signed, sealed and delivered in the presence of:

_____   _____
Witness #1 Signature

_____   Address:
Witness #1 Printed Name

_____
Witness #2 Signature

_____
Witness #2 Printed Name

STATE OF FLORIDA
COUNTY OF _____

The foregoing instrument was acknowledged before me this _____ day of _____, 20____, by _____, who is personally known to me or has produced _____ as identification.

_____
Notary Public

My Commission Expires:

Courtesy of Shari B. Olefson, Fowler White Boggs PA

APPENDIX G

SELLER AFFIDAVIT FORM

STATE OF FLORIDA

COUNTY OF _____

BEFORE ME, the undersigned authority, personally appeared _____ ("Affiant"), who, being duly sworn according to law, deposes and says as follows (as used in this Affidavit, the term "Affiant" shall include all parties executing this Affidavit):

1. That Affiant is the _____ of _____, a _____ ("Seller"), and as such has personal knowledge of the affairs of the Seller.
2. That Seller is the owner of the following described property situated in the County of _____, State of _____:

   See <u>Exhibit A</u>, attached hereto and made a part hereof

3. That, to the knowledge of Affiant, there are no parties who have any interest in said property other than Seller and there are no facts known to Affiant which could give rise to a claim being adversely asserted to any of said property, except: NONE
4. That Seller has not entered into any other agreement, contract or commitment for the sale, lease, mortgage, option or creation of any other encumbrance on said property except: NONE
5. That, to the knowledge of the Affiant, there are no taxes, liens or assessments due or about to become due which have attached or could attach to said property except: NONE
6. That Affiant is a citizen of the United States, of legal age, under no legal disabilities and has never been known by any name other than that shown above.

7. That Seller is in good standing under applicable laws and that the contemplated sale of said property by said entity is pursuant to proper authority.
8. That Affiant has the authority to execute any necessary conveyance documents on behalf of Seller and is in conformity with the Articles of Organization and/or the Operating Agreement of Seller.
9. That there are no actions or proceedings now pending in any State or Federal court to which Seller is a party including, but not limited to, proceedings in bankruptcy, receivership or insolvency, nor are there any judgments or liens of any nature which constitute or could constitute a charge or lien upon said property.
10. That, to the knowledge of Affiant, there have been no improvements, repairs, additions or alterations performed upon said property within the past ninety (90) days; that the Seller has not entered into any agreement or contract with any party for the furnishing of any labor, services or material in connection with any improvements, repairs, additions or alterations within the referenced time period; and that there are no parties who have any claim or right to a lien for services, labor or material in connection with any improvements, repairs, additions or alterations on said property.
11. That, to the knowledge of Affiant, the title commitment of _____ Title Insurance Company under No. _____ correctly and accurately reflects the status of the title to said property including all liens, mortgages and other encumbrances affecting said property.
12. Affiant makes this Affidavit for the purpose of inducing _____, as agent for _____ Title Insurance Company, to issue a policy of Title Insurance in connection with the above referenced transactions.

The foregoing instrument was acknowledged before me this _____ day of _____, 20_____, by _____, who is personally known to me or who has provided _____ as identification.

_____
Notary Public

My Commission Expires:

Courtesy of Shari B. Olefson, Fowler White Boggs PA

APPENDIX H

DUE DILIGENCE DISPOSITION CHECKLIST

Property Details	
Property Address	
Purchaser	
Seller	
Date	

Document	Due Diligence Documents at Acquisition	Update or documenta-tion due date	Reviewed prior to disclosure?	Not reviewed (provide reason)
1. Development consents and construction certificates				
2. Floor plans				
3. Certificates of occupancy for shell and tenant spaces				
4. Compliance certificates issued by any government authority				

5. Any other approvals issued by any government authority				
6. Current list of defects				
7. Schedule of expenses (showing reimbursements by tenants)				
8. Structural engineers' report				
9. Geotechnical report				
10. Environ-mental reports and follow-up				
11. Zoning compliance				
12. Certificates of business names, including business names intended to be transferred				

13. Reports re compliance with Codes and ADA				
14. Ownership entity, including joint venture documents, if any				
15. Tax calculation on High Level Gain/Loss				
16. Existing Title Policy and Survey, including Survey of any adjoining owned property and most current Survey				
17. Tenant files				
18. Existing loan documents, including release, prepayment penalties, assumption requirements and swap breakage costs				

19. Property management agreements, leasing agreements, and similar agreements				
20. Intellectual Property, including domain names, trademarks (including trademarks intended to be transferred), and website content				

II. Documents to be Disclosed to Purchaser

Document	Responsibility	Available	Not Available (reason)

1. Up-dated title commitment
 	
    Compare to title at acquisition
 	
    Review any CC&Rs for payment obligations and required approvals			

2. Tenancy Schedule The Tenancy Schedule must include a description of the premises occupied, the tenant's name, the nature of the occupancy (lease/license/holding over), the current rent/license fee, the lease term, details of any option, expiration date and whether a guarantee/security deposit is required under the lease.			
3. All current occupancy leases/licenses including car parking licenses and operating agreements. Include lease agreements and all amendments, licenses to occupy, variations, sub-leases, assignments, consents, letters of offer for new leases, improvement leases, licenses for communication aerials or other transmission facilities, documents and correspondence evidencing all incentive arrangements.			

4. Any other agreement under which a third party makes a payment to the owner (e.g.: Telco license or ATM license).			
5. Correspondence or documentation varying any of arrangements under #'s 3 and 4 (leases or otherwise). For example rent reductions, abatements, holding-over agreements. Include any documentation containing a right of first refusal over leasable area or any other pre-emptive rights.			
6. Schedule of Owner Security Deposits/ Letters of Credit/Performance Bonds/Guarantees (including location of originals of same).			
7. Receivables aging report			
8. List of fixtures and personal property included and excluded from sale			

9. Schedule of Service Contracts and existence of original Service Contracts The Service Contract Schedule must include a list of all services provided to the building, for example, maintenance of lifts and air-conditioning, cleaning contracts, plants, music etc and must include the term, costs, name of the contractor and termination rights.			
10. Signage/Logo Contracts			
11. Any agreements (adjoining owner, local authorities, third parties) not appearing on title			
12. Notices issued by municipality, EPA, water board or other statutory or govt. authorities.			

III. Information to be Provided to Purchaser

Information Required	Responsibility	Available	Not Available (reason)
1. Details of any litigation, disputes or pending problems (with regards to tenancies or other issues).			
2. Details of any amounts drawn under tenant security deposits.			
3. Details of any leases/licenses requiring a security for which no security is held.			
4. Details of any tenant's fit-out owned by the tenant.			
Building Works			
5. Details of any existing warranties and guarantees or defects liability period applicable in relation to the building and requirements for transfer, including inspection requirements and costs			
6. Details of any building works carried out since the last building certificate/survey.			

7. Details of any encroachments of the building (which are not shown on the survey)			
8. Details of any current proposed/ incomplete works for which development consent has been given.			
9. Details of any notice to complete issued by a government authority in relation to outstanding works.			
10. Details of any committed capital expenditure (e.g., outstanding commitment to a tenant, leasing commissions and other obligatons).			
Disputes (other than tenancies)			
11. Details of any litigation (e.g. in relation to easements, restrictive covenants, development consents etc) - existing or threatened.			

Associated Rights				
12. Details of any of the following: • Railway siding agreement • Pipeline or water supply agreements • Unregistered easements/rights of way • Airspace leases • Private streets • Other				
Affectations	Yes	No	Give Details	
13. Has any government authority notified owner or is owner otherwise aware, that the property is affected or is likely to become affected by any of the following: • Any sewer passing through the land • Any road proposal • Any railway proposal • Any heritage or conservation order • Any proposal by any authority to acquire the land • Any disputes re encroachments or common boundaries				

Courtesy of Joel D. Rubin, Seyfarth Shaw LLP

APPENDIX I

GENERAL CHECKLIST FOR CONSTRUCTION

Project Team and Disciplines

I. Overall Project Responsibility

   A. Unity of Command: who speaks with authority over the project? Identify major participants, lines of reporting and lines of authority.

      1. Architect
      2. Engineers
      3. Construction Managers/General Contractors
      4. Insurance consultants (for pre-construction) and claims contacts (for construction phase)
      5. Financing
      6. Project Rep
      7. Clerk of the Works
      8. Project Superintendent
      9. Chief of Safety

   B. Coordination: who oversees the process of document checking and coordination of disciplines? Who takes responsibility for the Construction Contract being an integrated, consistent written expression of the parties' deal?
   C. Zoning, Land Use, Expediting
   D. Vetting of information supplied by Owner. What standard of care and double-checking?
   E. Cost Control
   F. Scheduling. Determine whether a particular methodology will be mandated.
   G. Strategy.

      1. Project Delivery Method
      2. Fast-track for speed to market
      3. Fast-track to control costs
      4. Other special strategic concerns

APPENDICES

II. Pre-Design

    A. Programming

        1. Project Concept
        2. Preliminary feasibility studies
        3. Canvas for Government Incentive Programs

    B. Site Selection

        1. Already-owned
        2. To be acquired
        3. Zoning and land use

    C. Site Services

        1. Utilities
        2. Title and acquisition. Surveys
        3. Zoning and land use
        4. Existing uses and improvements
        5. Phase I environmental
        6. Geotechnical studies if indicated

    D. Design Team

        1. Design Architect
        2. Project Architect
        3. Structural Engineer
        4. Mechanical Engineer
        5. Civil Engineer
        6. Landscape Architect
        7. Interior Design
        8. Special Design
            Specify Type: (Kitchen, bath, display, security, etc.)
        9. Special Studies
            Specify Type (Materials research, special means & methods, exotic construction, etc.)

E. Project Delivery System

    1. Design-Bid-Build

        a. Fixed Price
        b. Cost Plus with GMP
        c. Cost Plus without GMP

    2. Construction Management

        a. As Agent for Owner
        b. CM At Risk

III. With GMP

  A. Without GMP

    1. Multi-Prime Contract (Wicks Law)
    2. Design-Build
    3. Fast-Track

  B. Dispute Resolution

    1. Arbitration? Which forum/rules?
    2. Mediation? Forum/rules
    3. Litigation: what forum?
    4. In all cases

        a. Pending resolution terms?
        b. Provision for consolidation and impleader

  C. Security

    1. Performance Bonds/Subguard
    2. Payment Bonds
    3. Letters of Credit/Independent Bank Guaranties
    4. Retainage

APPENDICES

D. Insurance

1. Election whether to employ wrap-up coverage
2. Project Policy for design professionals?
3. Develop insurance program as an element of overall project risk management and enforce compliance
4. Ensure coordination between terms of insurance required by contracts and coverage actually obtained.

IV. Design Phase

1. Ensure project schedule is established and adhered-to
2. Monitor submissions, cross-checking and stops for owner/lender et c. approval
3. Ensure cost estimating services are kept up to date and monitor for potential need to engage in value engineering.

V. Contract Award

1. Competitive Bid Based on 100% Design?
2. Competitive Tender Based on 90+% Design?
3. RFPs to be followed by negotiation
4. Letters of Intent/Early Start Agreement

    a. Incorporate Agreement to Provide Insurance
    b. Waivers of Subrogation
    c. Indemnification Agreements

VI. Construction

1. Ensure all required documents (insurance certs, hold harmless agreements, et c.) are filed when work begins by withholding payment until filing accomplished.
2. Ensure that someone actually looks at the filed documents,
3. Consider legal review of change orders, especially when based on claims or for significant $$.
4. Oversee operation of dispute resolution techniques

        a. Preliminary determination by umpire
        b. Final determination by ADR or Judge.
        c. Potential intermediate review by "board pof changes," true neutral umpire, etc.

VIII. Closeout

    A. Coordinate consents of sureties to release retainage
    B. Identify pending claims
    C. Verify Non-Construction Completion:

        1. Training
        2. Commissioning
        3. Certificate of Occupancy/Public Assembly License
        4. Warranties
        5. Attic stock, manuals, tools, test equipment

    D. Verify final releases of lien rights

Courtesy of Kevin J. Connolly, Anderson Kill & Olick PC

APPENDIX J

OWNER'S CHECKLIST FOR RESPONDING TO NEW YORK MECHANICS' LIENS

New York's lien law is complex to a degree that many losses can be traced to a lack of awareness of what to do next. These steps are also useful, when adapted, for other states that have elaborate lien regimes.

I. Tender

    A. Review all pertinent documents to ascertain parties that have a duty to (a) secure discharge of the lien or (b) to defend against its foreclosure.

        1. Typical documents include ground leases, space leases, development agreements, mortgages.
        2. Ascertain conditions precedent to client's right to invoke remedies, recover attorneys fees and costs.

    B. Tender defense of action or demand discharge of lien versus all potentially-responsible parties.

    C. If no such party identified or if all such parties fail and refuse to discharge the lien and/or defend the action, consider costs and benefits of filing a bond to discharge the lien or settling with the lienor.

II. Responding to the Notice of Lien

    A. Review for facial compliance with Lien Law.

        1. Verify public or private improvement.
        2. Review four corners of Notice of Lien.
        3. Verify correctness of legal description. Cross-check versus underlying documents (IA1).
        4. Verify in/correct nomenclature of Owner (Lien Law §§2(3), (4), (5); 13(5)

5. Confirm Service of Notice of Lien on Owner (Lien Law §11)
6. Confirm filing of Affidavit of Service of Lien within 35 days after filing (§11)

B. Maintain non-responsibility to remote lienors by complying strictly with §8 of the Lien Law.
C. Demand itemized statement under §38 of the Lien Law. Note highly-accelerated motion to expunge lien if demand not complied-with. Also serves as a super demand for bill of particulars while preserving the right to serve interrogatories.
D. Consider serving a demand to commence foreclosure within 30 days under §59 (penalty for willful exaggeration cannot be imposed absent trial of a foreclosure action).

§2(3). Owner. The term "owner," when used in this chapter, includes the owner in fee of real property, or of a less estate therein, a lessee for a term of years, a vendee in possession under a contract for the purchase of such real property, and all persons having any right, title or interest in such real property, which may be sold under an execution in pursuance of the provisions of statutes relating to the enforcement of liens of judgment, and all persons having any right or franchise granted by a public corporation to use the streets and public places thereof, and any right, title or interest in and to such franchise. The purchaser of real property at a statutory or judicial sale shall be deemed the owner thereof from the time of such sale. If the purchaser at such sale fails to complete the purchase, pursuant to the terms of the sale, all liens created by his consent after such sale shall be a lien on any deposit made by him and not on the real property sold.

§2(4). Improvement. The term "improvement," when used in this chapter, includes the demolition, erection, alteration or repair of any structure upon, connected with, or beneath the surface of, any real property and any work done upon such property or materials furnished for its permanent improvement, and shall also include any work done or materials furnished in equipping any such structure with any chandeliers, brackets or other fixtures or apparatus for supplying gas or electric light and shall also include the drawing by any architect or engineer or surveyor, of any plans or specifications or survey, which are prepared for or used in connection with such improvement and shall also include the value of materials actually manufactured for but not delivered to the real property, and shall also include the reasonable rental value for the period of actual use of machinery, tools and equipment and the value of compressed gases furnished for welding or cutting in connection with the demolition, erection, alteration or repair of any real property, and the value of fuel and lubricants consumed by machinery operating on the improvement, or by motor vehicles owned, operated or controlled by the owner, or a contractor or subcontractor while engaged exclusively in the transportation of materials to or from the improvement for the purposes thereof and shall also include the performance of real estate brokerage services in obtaining a lessee for a term of more than three years of all or any part of real property to be used for other than residential purposes pursuant to a written contract of brokerage employment or compensation.

§2(5). Cost of improvement. The term "cost of improvement," when used in this chapter, means expenditures incurred by the owner in paying the claims of a contractor, an architect, engineer or surveyor, a subcontractor, laborer and materialman, arising out of the improvement, and in paying the amount of taxes based on payrolls including such persons and withheld or required to be withheld and taxes based on the purchase price or value of materials or equipment required to be installed or furnished in connection with the performance of the improvement, payment of taxes and unemployment insurance and other contributions due by reason of the employment out of which any such claim arose, and payment of any benefits or wage supplements or the amounts necessary to provide such benefits or furnish such supplements, to the extent that the owner, as employer, is obligated to pay or provide such benefits or furnish such supplements by any agreement to which he is a party, and shall also include fair and reasonable sums paid for obtaining building loan and subsequent financing, premiums on bond or bonds filed pursuant to section thirty-seven of this chapter or required by any such building loan contract or by any lease to be mortgaged pursuant thereto, or required by any mortgage to be subordinated to the building loan mortgage, premiums on bond or bonds filed to discharge liens, sums paid to take by assignment prior existing mortgages, which are consolidated with building loan mortgages and also the interest charges on such mortgages, sums paid to discharge or reduce the indebtedness under mortgages and accrued interest thereon and other encumbrances upon real estate existing prior to the time when the lien provided for in this chapter may attach, sums paid to discharge building loan mortgages whenever recorded, taxes, assessments and water rents existing prior to the commencement of the improvement, and also those accruing during the making of the improvement, and interest on building loan mortgages, ground rent and premiums on insurance likewise accruing during the making of the improvement. The application of the proceeds of any building loan mortgage or other mortgage to reimburse the owner for any payments made for any of the above mentioned items for said improvement prior to the date of the initial advance received under the building loan mortgage or other mortgage shall be deemed to be an expenditure within the "cost of improvement" as above defined; provided, however, such payments are itemized in the building loan contract and/or other mortgage other than a building loan mortgage, and provided further, that the payments have been made subsequent to the commencement of the improvement.

§13 (5) No instrument of conveyance recorded subsequent to the commencement of the improvement, and before the expiration of the period specified in section ten of this chapter for filing of notice of lien after the completion of the improvement, shall be valid as against liens filed within a corresponding period of time measured from the recording of such conveyance, unless the instrument contains a covenant by the grantor that he will receive the consideration for such conveyance and will hold the right to receive such consideration as a trust fund to be applied first for the purpose of paying the cost of the improvement and that he will apply the same first to the payment of the cost of the improvement before using any part of the total of the same for any other purpose. Nothing in this subdivision shall be construed as imposing upon the grantee any obligation to see to the proper application of such consideration by the grantor. Nothing in this subdivision shall apply to a deed given by a referee or other person appointed by the court for the sole purpose of selling real property. Nothing in this subdivision shall apply to the consideration received by a grantor who, pursuant to a written agreement entered into and duly recorded prior to the commencement of the improvement, conveys to the person making such improvement, the land upon which such improvement is made. However, such a conveyance shall be subject to liens filed prior thereto, as provided by this chapter. To the extent that the trust res consists of the right to receive the consideration for such conveyance as distinct from the consideration actually received, breach of the trust shall give rise to a civil action only. The covenant provided for herein shall be deemed to have been made and to be in full force and effect if, in lieu of the foregoing provisions, a statement in substantially the following form is contained in the instrument of conveyance, "subject to the trust fund provisions of section thirteen of the lien law." Except that this section shall not apply to any mortgage taken by the home owners' loan corporation, a corporation created under an act of congress, known as the "home owners' loan act of nineteen hundred thirty-three," and the "home owners' loan act of nineteen hundred thirty-three as amended," and said mortgage shall have priority over any and all liens filed subsequent to the date of the recording of said mortgage whether or not the cash and/or bonds for which said mortgage has been taken as security, shall have been advanced at the time of the execution of such mortgage or subsequent thereto, and it shall not be necessary to execute and file any building loan contract or any other contract, in compliance with this section or any part thereof.

§8. Terms of contract may be demanded. A statement of the terms of a contract made between an owner and a contractor, pursuant to which an improvement of real property is being made, and, of the amount due or to become due thereon shall be furnished upon demand in writing by the owner, or his duly authorized agent, to a subcontractor, laborer or material man performing labor for or furnishing materials to a contractor, or subcontractor, under such contract. If, within thirty days of such demand the owner refuses or neglects to furnish such statement or falsely states the terms of such contract or the amount due or to become due thereon, and a subcontractor, laborer or material man has not been paid the amount of his claim against a contractor or subcontractor, under such contract, and a judgment has been obtained and execution issued against such contractor or subcontractor and returned wholly or partly unsatisfied, *the owner shall be liable for the loss sustained by reason of such refusal, neglect or false statement, and the lien of such subcontractor, laborer or material man, filed as prescribed in this article, against the real property improved for the labor performed or materials furnished after such demand, shall exist to the same extent and be enforced in the same manner as if such labor and materials had been directly performed for and furnished to such owner.*

§11 (part)

Failure to file proof of such a service with the county clerk within thirty-five days after the notice of lien is filed shall terminate the notice as a lien.

Courtesy of Kevin J. Connolly, Anderson Kill & Olick PC

APPENDIX K

LOAN CLOSING CHECKLIST

$_____ LOAN

FROM

_____ BANK

TO

_____

(PROJECT NAME)

CONTACT INFORMATION

Lender (L)	LENDER'S COUNSEL (LC)
_____ @ .com	Jane B. Morgan www.watkinseager.com
Address:	Address: Watkins & Eager PLLC 400 East Capitol Street Jackson, MS 39201
Phone #:	Phone #: 601.965.1900
Fax #:	Fax #: 601.965.1901
Borrower (B)	**Borrower's Counsel (BC)**
_____ @ .com	_____ @ .com
Address:	Address:
Phone #:	Phone #:
Fax #:	Fax #:
Title Company (TC)	**Lender's Inspector**
_____ @ .com	_____ @ .com
Firm:	Firm:
Address:	Address:
Phone #:	Phone #:
Fax #:	Fax #:

PROPERTY INFORMATION

Project Name:
Address:
County/Jurisdiction:
Parcel ID:

_____ **BANK**

(FILE NO: _____)

	DOCUMENT	RESPONSIBILITY	STATUS
I.	**LOAN DOCUMENTS**		
1.	Promissory Note	LC	
2.	Loan Agreement	LC	
3.	Deed of Trust, Security Agreement and Fixture Filing	LC	
4.	Assignment of Leases, Rents and Profits	LC	
5.	Unconditional Guaranty Agreements (a) (b) (c)	LC	
6.	Security Agreement	LC	
7.	Assignment of Plans, Specifications, Permits and Contracts	LC	
8.	SNDA/Estoppel Certificates	LC	
9.	Subordination Agreements	LC	
10.	UCC-1 Financing Statements– County/State	LC	
11.	Certificate of Borrower	LC	
12.	Borrower's Attorney Opinion Letter	BC (LC to offer form)	

APPENDICES

II.	**TITLE/SURVEY**		
13.	Title Insurance Commitment/Proforma Policy (please see Title Insurance Requirements provided by LC) (a) copies of all title exception instruments	B/BC/TC	
14.	Survey (please see Survey Requirements provided by LC)	B/BC	
15.	Owner's/Contractor's Affidavit	B/BC/TC	
16.	Certificate of Release/UCC-3 Termination Statement(s)	B/BC/TC	
17.	Escrow Instruction Letter to the Title Company	LC/TC	
18.	Closing Protection Letter (if applicable)	TC	
19.	Settlement/Closing Statement	B/BC/L/TC	
20.	Wiring Instructions for Title Company	TC	

III.	**PROJECT INFORMATION**		
21.	Appraisal	L/B	
22.	Phase I Environmental Assessment Report	L/B	
23.	Project Plans & Specifications (a) approvals by applicable gov. agencies	B/BC	

24.	Project Budget	B/BC	
25.	AIA Fixed Price Construction Contract	B/BC	
26.	List of Sub-Contractors (over $_____)	B/BC	
27.	General Contractor's Payment & Performance Bond	B/BC	
28.	Owner/Architect Agreement	B/BC	
29.	Engineer's Contract	B/BC	
30.	Soil Report	B/BC	
31.	Copies of Project Permits (a) Grading/Demolition Permit(s) (b) Building Permit(s)	B/BC	
32.	Zoning Confirmation Letter	B/BC	
33.	Utility Availability Letters (a) Electricity (b) Gas (c) Sewer/Water	B/BC	
34.	Flood Hazard Certificate	L	
35.	General Liability Insurance Certificate (ACORD 27 form, naming lender as Additional Insured)	B/BC	
36.	Builder's Risk/Hazard Insurance (ACORD 27 form, naming lender as Mortgagee/Loss Payee)	B/BC	

37.	Copies of Current Leases/Form of Lease (a) Estoppel Certificate(s)	B/BC	
38.	Commitment Letter from Permanent Lender	B/BC	
IV.	**ENTITY INFORMATION**		
39.	As to the Borrower – (_____) Certificate of Formation/Limited Partnership (_) Operating/Partnership Agreement (_) Certificate of Existence (_) Certificate of Good Standing (_) Qualification to Transact Business, if applicable (_) Tax Identification Number (_) UCC, Tax Lien and Judgment Searches (state & local) (_)	B/BC	
40.	As to the Manager/Member/General Partner – (_____) Certificate of Formation/Limited Partnership (_) Operating/Partnership Agreement (_) Certificate of Existence (_) Certificate of Good Standing (_) Qualification to Transact Business, if applicable (_) Tax Identification Number (_) UCC, Tax Lien and Judgment Searches (state & local) (_)	B/BC	

41.	*[Insert others as applicable]*	B/BC	
42.	As to the Guarantor – (_____) Certificate of Formation/Limited Partnership (_) Operating/Partnership Agreement (_) Certificate of Existence (_) Certificate of Good Standing (_) Qualification to Transact Business, if applicable (_) Tax Identification Number (_) UCC, Tax Lien and Judgment Searches (state & local) (_)	B/BC	
43.	*[Insert others as applicable]*		
44.	Financial Statements of Borrower and Guarantor	B/BC	

V.	**POST-CLOSING ITEMS**[1]		
45.	Recordation of Warranty Deed (if applicable) and Deed of Trust	BC/TC	
46.	Filing of UCC-1 Financing Statements (obtain file-stamped copy)	BC/TC	
47.	Title Update/Final Title Policy	BC/TC	

This Closing Checklist is provided as a convenience to the parties to the above transaction and in no way modifies the requirements imposed by the Lender pursuant to the Commitment Letter, the Loan Documents or Lender's standard lending procedures. Lender reserves the right to modify and amend this Closing Checklist at any time.

Courtesy of Jane B. Morgan, Watkins & Eager PLLC

APPENDIX L

STATUTORY ACKNOWLEDGMENT FORMS

The following forms of acknowledgment may be used in the State of Mississippi for conveyances or other written instruments affecting real estate or personal property for the corporate structure indicated. Upon execution and prior to recording any document in the land records, the real estate attorney should carefully check the form of acknowledgment to ensure that it is properly signed and sealed by the notary and in recordable form. Note the distinction made in these statutory forms between member-managed and manager-managed limited liability companies.

Miss Code Ann. 89-3-7 (d): In the case of a corporate member of a member-managed limited liability company:

STATE OF _____
COUNTY OF_____

Personally appeared before me, the undersigned authority in and for the said county and state, on this_____ day of _____, 20_____, within my jurisdiction, the within named _____, who acknowledged to me that (he) (she)is _____ of _____, a _____ corporation and member of_____, a _____ member-managed limited liability company, and that for and on behalf of said corporation as member of said limited liability company, and as the act and deed of said corporation as member of said limited liability company, and as the act and deed of said limited liability company, (he) (she) executed the above and foregoing instrument, after first having been duly authorized by said corporation and said limited liability company so to do.

_____ (NOTARY PUBLIC)

My commission expires: _____ (Affix official seal, if applicable)

Miss Code Ann. 89-3-7 (e): In the case of a corporate manager of a manager-managed limited liability company:

STATE OF _____
COUNTY OF_____

Personally appeared before me, the undersigned authority in and for the said county and state, on this_____ day of_____, 20_____, within my jurisdiction, the within named_____, who acknowledged to me that (he) (she)is_____ of_____, a _____ corporation and manager of_____, a_____ manager-managed limited liability company, and that for and on behalf of said corporation as manager of said limited liability company, and as the act and deed of said corporation as manager of said limited liability company, and as the act and deed of said limited liability company, (he) (she)executed the above and foregoing instrument, after first having been duly authorized by said corporation and said limited liability company so to do.

_____ (NOTARY PUBLIC)

My commission expires: _____ (Affix official seal, if applicable)

Courtesy of Jane B. Morgan, Watkins & Eager PLLC

APPENDIX M

EARLY ACCESS AGREEMENT FORM

This ACCESS AGREEMENT (this "Agreement") is entered into as of this _____ day of _____, ____ (the "Effective Date") by and between _____, a _____ (hereinafter referred to as "Licensor"), and _____, a _____ (hereinafter referred to as "Licensee").

W I T N E S S E T H:

WHEREAS, Licensor is the fee owner of certain real property consisting of approximately _____ acres located in _____ (the "Property"); and

WHEREAS, Licensee contemplates the acquisition of the Property, and the development and construction of _____ on the Property; and

WHEREAS, Licensor and Licensee are in the process of negotiating or intend to commence the negotiation of a purchase and sale agreement for the Property (the "Purchase Agreement"); and

WHEREAS, Licensee desires to commence the Work (as hereinafter defined) on the Property and has requested that Licensor grant to Licensee a license to enter upon the Property for the purposes set forth herein in order to commence the Work; and

WHEREAS, Licensor is willing to grant Licensee and its authorized representatives the right of entry on and access to the Property to perform the Work as set forth below (the "License");

NOW, THEREFORE, in consideration of Ten and No/100 Dollars ($10.00) and other good and valuable consideration, the receipt and sufficiency of which are hereby acknowledged, the parties hereto agree as follows:

1. <u>Grant of License</u>. Licensor hereby grants to Licensee, its representatives and its agents, a license and right to access and enter upon the Property in order to inspect, test and examine the Property, and to perform environmental and wetlands assessments, topographical surveys, geotechnical studies, soil tests, drillings, borings, percolation tests and other tests needed to determine environmental, surface, subsurface and topographic conditions, the availability of utilities and other matters deemed necessary or appropriate by Licensee with respect to the Property (collectively, the "Work"); provided, however, that Licensee shall return the Property after said entry and testing to substantially its condition prior thereto. Licensor represents and warrants to Licensee that Licensee is duly authorized to grant the License for access provided herein to Licensee.

2. <u>Indemnification</u>. Licensee hereby agrees to indemnify, defend and hold harmless Licensor from and against any and all liabilities, damages, expenses, causes of action, suits, claims or judgments arising from the exercise of the License rights granted hereunder and the activities related thereto. Licensee further indemnifies and holds harmless Licensor from and against any and all claims for liens and any actions, suits, claims or judgments relating to any such liens which may arise out of any work performed by or under the direction of Licensee on the Property or any materials or services furnished in connection therewith. Notwithstanding the foregoing, Licensee's agreement to defend, indemnify and hold harmless as set forth above shall not apply to any claims, demands, penalties, fines, liabilities, costs or expenses, or attorneys' fees, arising out of or related to (i) any condition upon or under the Property not caused by Licensee or that existed prior to the commencement of Licensee's investigations, (ii) any violation of law existing with respect to the Property not caused by Licensee, or (iii) the acts, omissions or negligence of Licensor, its employees, agents, servants or independent contractors.

3. <u>Insurance</u>. At all times during the term of this License, Licensee shall cause its agents to maintain commercial general liability insurance against claims for personal injury, death or property

damage occurring on the Property to afford protection to the limit of not less than _____ Dollars ($_____) with respect to injury or death of a single person, and to the limit of not less than _____ Dollars ($_____) in the aggregate, and to the limit of _____ Dollars ($_____) with respect to property damage, against claims for personal injury, death or property damage occurring upon, in or about the Property and arising out of the exercise of this License.

4. <u>Not a Public Dedication.</u> The License is not, and shall not be deemed to be, a public dedication, and no party shall have any rights in, to or under the License except as expressly permitted or granted hereunder. The License shall not be filed or recorded by either party.

5. <u>No Obligation Implied.</u> Either Licensor or Licensee may withdraw at any time from discussions or negotiations regarding the Purchase Agreement. Licensee acknowledges and agrees that Licensee is proceeding with its due diligence, including, without limitation, the Work, at Licensee's own risk and expense. Neither the execution of this Agreement nor the exercise of the rights granted hereby shall imply, infer or impose any obligation upon Licensor or Licensee to negotiate or enter into any agreement with respect to the Property. Any such obligations will arise, if at all, only when the Purchase Agreement for the Property is executed by Licensor and Licensee, and shall be governed by any such agreement.

6. <u>Confidentiality.</u> Licensor agrees to hold the information contained in this Agreement or any other instrument or agreement which may be entered into in connection with the transaction contemplated hereby (collectively, the "Transaction Documents") in strict confidence and not to disclose any term or condition contained in this Agreement, the Transaction Documents or any reports or documents prepared in connection with the Work, to any person or entity other than the respective attorneys, accountants and consultants of Licensor (all of whom shall also agree to such confidentiality). Licensor and Licensee acknowledge and agree that this provision shall not be deemed breached if disclosure is

required by applicable law or is otherwise consented to by Licensee. This paragraph shall survive the expiration or termination of this Agreement.

7. <u>Governing Law</u>. This Agreement shall be construed, interpreted and enforced in accordance with the laws of the State of _____.

8. <u>Counterparts</u>. This Agreement may be executed in two or more counterparts, each of which shall be deemed to be an original, and all of which counterparts when taken together shall constitute one and the same instrument.

9. <u>Authority</u>. By their respective signatures that follow, the parties executing this Agreement on behalf of Licensor and Licensee acknowledge, represent and warrant that they have been authorized to do so by all necessary action to execute and deliver this Agreement.

IN WITNESS WHEREOF, the parties have executed and delivered this Agreement as of the day and year first above written.

LICENSOR:

_____, a _____
By:_____
Name: _____
Title: _____

LICENSEE:

_____, a _____
By:_____
Name: _____
Title: _____

Courtesy of Kwame A. Benjamin, Seyfarth Shaw LLP

APPENDIX N

DUE DILIGENCE CHECKLIST

SELLER: _____, a
_____ ("S")

SELLER'S COUNSEL: _____ ("SC")

PURCHASER: _____, a
_____ ("P")

PURCHASER'S COUNSEL: _____ ("PC")

CONTRACT: _____

TITLE/ESCROW AGENT: _____

BROKER: _____

PROPERTY: _____

PURCHASE PRICE: $_____

TARGET CLOSING DATE: _____

OUTSIDE CLOSING DATE: _____

A. CONTRACT		
1. Agreement for the Sale and Purchase of Real Estate	P&S	
2. Amendments to Agreement for the Sale and Purchase of Real Estate	P&S	
3. Verification of Earnest Money Deposits	P&S	
4. Assignment of Real Property Purchase Agreement	P	
B. AUTHORIZATION OF SELLER		
1. Tax Identification Number	S	
2. Certificate of Existence	S/SC	
3. Articles of Incorporation	S/SC	
4. Bylaws	S/SC	
5. Unanimous Consent/Resolution	S/SC	

C. AUTHORIZATION OF PURCHASER		
1. Tax Identification Number	P	
2. Certificate of Existence	P/PC	
3. Certificate of Organization	P/PC	
4. Operating Agreement	P/PC	
5. Members Consents (if applicable)	P/PC	
D. DELIVERY OF SELLER'S DELIVERABLE ITEMS		
1. Tax Bills for Property	S	
2. Environmental and Soils Reports	S	
3. Surveys, Plats, Site Plans and Topographical Maps	S	
4. Other Seller Deliverables Per Contract	S	
E. TITLE		
1. Existing Owner's Title Insurance Policy	S/SC	
2. Commitment for Title Insurance	PC	
3. Title Exceptions (including appurtenant easements)	PC	
4. Tax Report/Property Tax Information	P/PC	
5. Lien Waivers (if applicable)	P/PC	
6. Payoff Letter (if applicable)	P/PC	
7. Release Instruments (if applicable)	S/SC/P/PC	
8. "Marked" Commitment for Title Insurance with endorsements	PC	
9. Title Objection Letter	PC	
10. Exhibit A (Legal Description)	P/PC	
11. Exhibit B (Permitted Title Exceptions)	P/PC	
12. Verification that any appurtenant easements are insured	P/PC	

13. Policy of Title Insurance (ALTA Form B 1992-standard printed exceptions deleted)	P/PC	
14. Endorsements to Policy of Title Insurance	P/PC	
15. Title Insurance Affidavits	S/SC	
16. Insured Closing Letter	P/PC	
F. SURVEY/SITE PLAN		
1. ALTA/ACSM Land Title Survey	P	
2. Surveyor Inspection Report	P	
3. Surveyor Certificate	P	
4. Survey Objection Letter	P/PC	
5. Subdivision Plat (if applicable)	S/SC	
6. Conceptual/Preliminary Site Plan	P/PC	
7. Final Site Plan	P/PC	
G. INSURANCE		
1. Commercial General Liability Insurance Policy (with broad form endorsement)	P	
2. Loss of Rents Insurance Policy	P	
3. Commercial Property Insurance Policy (written on "all-risk" basis) (a) Builder's Risk	P	
4. Flood Insurance Policy (if applicable)	P	
H. DUE DILIGENCE		
1. Evidence of zoning compliance, all other compliance letters and description of existing zoning on Property	P/PC (and local counsel if required)	
2. Zoning Certificate	P/PC	
3. Rezoning Application	P/PC	

4. Evidence of Utilities
  (a) Sewer
  (b) Water
  (c) Gas
  (d) Telephone
  (e) Electric
  (f) Drainage (Storm Sewer)
  (g) Fire Protection-Sprinkler System
	P/PC	

5. Containment Letters	P/PC	
6. Appraisal	P/PC	
7. Phase I Environmental Report (updated and certified)	P/PC	
8. Phase I Environmental Reliance Letter	P/PC	
9. Geotechnical Report	P/PC	
10. Geotechnical Reliance Letter	P/PC	
11. Wetlands Report (if applicable)	P/PC	
12. Verification of Flood Zone and Existing Flood Insurance/Flood Maps (if applicable)	P/PC	
13. Sewer Permits	P/PC	
14. Building Permits	P/PC	
15. Land Disturbance/Grading Permits	P/PC	
16. Other Permits/Warranties	P/PC	
17. Final Site Plan Approval	P/PC	
18. Project Budget	P/PC	
19. General Contractor Agreement and certifications	P/PC	
20. Engineer's Contract and certifications	P/PC	
21. Architect's Contract and certifications	P/PC	
22. Management Agreement	P/PC	
23. Development Agreement	P/PC	
24. List of Plans and Specifications	P/PC	

I. CLOSING DOCUMENTS

1. Deed	PC	
2. Transfer Tax Form	PC	
3. Quitclaim Deed (if required)	PC	
4. Seller's Affidavit	PC	
5. Certificate of Non-Foreign Status	PC	
6. Affidavit of Seller's Residence	PC	
7. IRS Form 1099	PC	
8. Certificate of Representations and Warranties	PC	
9. Bill of Sale	PC	
10. Broker's Lien Waiver	PC	
11. "GAP" Indemnity Agreement for Title Company (if applicable)	PC	
12. Settlement Statement	P/PC	

J. LOAN DOCUMENTS

1. Commitment Letter/Term Sheet	P	
2. Promissory Note	P/PC	
3. Mortgage/Deed of Trust/Deed to Secure Debt	P/PC	
4. Assignment of Leases and Rents	P/PC	
5. Loan Agreement	P/PC	
6. Environmental Indemnity Agreement	P/PC	
7. Payment Guaranty	P/PC	
8. Completion Guaranty	P/PC	
9. Borrower's Affidavit	P/PC	
10. Opinion Letter (local counsel if required)	P/PC	
11. UCC Financing Statements	P/PC	
12. Other Loan Documents	P/PC	

K. EQUITY DOCUMENTS

1. Investment Summary	P/PC	
2. Equity Amount	P/PC	
3. Contribution/Indemnity Agreements	P/PC	

L. ORGANIZATIONAL DOCUMENTS		
1. JV Level – See Section C	P/PC	
2. Partners Operating Agreement	P/PC	
3. Partners Certificate of Organization	P/PC	
4. Development Operating Agreement	P/PC	
5. Development Certificate of Organization	P/PC	
6. Restricted Member Agreement	P/PC	
7. Resolutions/Consents – all entities	P/PC	

Courtesy of Kwame A. Benjamin, Seyfarth Shaw LLP

APPENDIX O

REAL PROPERTY PURCHASE AGREEMENT

by and between

_____, as Seller

and

_____, as Purchaser

THIS REAL PROPERTY PURCHASE AGREEMENT (hereinafter sometimes referred to as the "Agreement") is hereby made and entered into as of the Effective Date (as hereinafter defined) by and between _____ (hereinafter referred to as the "Seller"), and _____ (hereinafter sometimes referred to as the "Purchaser").

WITNESSETH THAT:

WHEREAS, Seller desires to sell and Purchaser desires to purchase, upon the terms and conditions hereinafter set forth, that certain tract or parcel of land containing approximately _____ acres of land located at _____, in _____ County, _____, as described on Exhibit A attached hereto, together with all rights, easements and appurtenances pertaining thereto and all improvements, trees, bushes, landscaping and foliage thereon (collectively, the "Property");

NOW, THEREFORE, in consideration of the mutual promises and covenants contained herein and other good and valuable consideration, the receipt and sufficiency of which are all hereby acknowledged by each of the parties hereto, the parties hereto agree as follows:

1. Purchase Price. Subject to and pursuant to the following terms and conditions, Seller shall sell and transfer the Property to Purchaser and Purchaser shall purchase the Property from Seller and pay to

Seller the sum of _____ ($_____) (hereinafter sometimes referred to as the "<u>Purchase Price</u>"), by the delivery of immediately available and collectible funds, less the Earnest Money (as hereinafter defined) and subject to adjustment as provided herein.

2. <u>Earnest Money</u>.

    a. <u>Deposit of Earnest Money</u>. Within _____ (__) days after the execution of this Agreement, Purchaser agrees to deposit in escrow with the national business unit of _____ (the "<u>Title Company</u>") an earnest money deposit of _____ and No/100 Dollars ($_____) (the "<u>Earnest Money</u>"). Purchaser may, at its option, direct the Title Company to invest said Earnest Money in an interest bearing account designated by Purchaser. All Earnest Money held in escrow by the Title Company pursuant to this Paragraph 2, together with any additional deposits of Earnest Money if made pursuant to this Agreement, shall be applied for Purchaser's benefit against the Purchase Price of the Property at Closing of the purchase of the Property or as otherwise provided for by this Agreement. All interest which has accrued on the Earnest Money deposited with the Title Company shall, under all circumstances, belong to Purchaser (unless the earnest money is forfeited by Purchaser pursuant to the terms of this Agreement, in which case the interest on the earnest money will go to Seller along with the forfeited earnest money. If the Purchaser shall validly and timely exercise any right under this Agreement to terminate this Agreement prior to Closing, the Earnest Money, together with any and all interest accrued thereon, shall be immediately paid over and refunded to Purchaser whereupon this Agreement shall be of no further force and effect, and the parties hereto shall have no further rights, duties or obligations hereunder. The Title Company shall make disbursements of the Earnest Money held by it in accordance with this Agreement and in reliance upon written directions of Purchaser and Seller.

b. <u>Disputes Regarding Earnest Money</u>. In the event that a dispute arises with respect to the distribution of any funds held, the Title Company may apply to a court of competent jurisdiction for an order determining the party or parties to whom such deposit shall be paid. All costs of such proceedings together with all reasonable attorney's fees and costs incurred by the Title Company and the successful party or parties in connection therewith shall be paid by the unsuccessful party or parties to such proceeding. In performing its duties as Escrow Agent holding the Earnest Money as provided in this Agreement, the Title Company shall not incur any liability to anyone for any damages, losses or expenses, except for willful default or breach of trust, and it shall accordingly not incur any such liability with respect (a) to any action taken or omitted in good faith upon advice of its counsel, or (b) to any action taken or omitted in reliance upon any instrument, including written notice or instruction provided for in this Agreement, not only as to its due execution and the validity and effectiveness of its provisions, but also as to the truth and accuracy of any information contained therein, which Title Company shall in good faith believe to be genuine, to have been signed or presented by a proper person or persons, and to conform with the provisions of this Agreement. In the event of a dispute between any of the parties hereto sufficient in the discretion of Title Company to justify its doing so, Title Company shall be entitled to tender into the registry or custody of any court of competent jurisdiction, the Earnest Money held under this Agreement, together with such legal pleadings as it deems appropriate, and thereupon be discharged from all further duties and liabilities under this Agreement. Any such legal action may be brought in such court as Title Company shall determine to have jurisdiction thereof.

3. Purchaser's Inspections.

   a. <u>Inspection Period</u>. Purchaser, its agents and representatives, shall have at all times until _____ (____) days from the date of full execution of this Agreement ("<u>Inspection Period</u>"), and thereafter until Closing if this Agreement has not been terminated pursuant to the terms hereof, to enter upon the Property, including, without limitation, any improvements located thereon, in order to inspect and examine same and perform topographical surveys, soil tests, borings, percolation tests and other tests needed to determine surface, subsurface and topographic conditions. To the extent that any testing disturbs the surface of the Property, Purchaser will, at the expense of Purchaser, restore the Property to as nearly as possible its condition prior to the testing. Purchaser hereby indemnifies Seller and agrees to hold Seller harmless from and against any loss, damage, personal injury, death, property damage, liens, liabilities or expense of any nature whatsoever, including, without limitation, reasonable attorneys' fees actually incurred, which Seller may suffer or incur as a result of the exercise by Purchaser of its rights under this Paragraph 3.

   b. <u>Extension of Inspection Period</u>. Purchaser shall have the right to extend the Inspection Period for an additional period of _____ (____) days upon written notice by Purchaser to Seller given prior to the expiration of the Inspection Period and upon the payment of an additional Earnest Money deposit of _____ and No/100 Dollars ($_____), which additional Earnest Money deposit shall be deposited with Title Company within _____ (____) days of the date of Purchaser's election to extend the Inspection Period hereunder and shall become a part of the Earnest Money and shall be applied against the Purchase Price at Closing or otherwise distributed with all other Earnest Money pursuant to this Agreement.

c. <u>Conditions During Inspection Period</u>. It is specifically understood that Purchaser intends to improve and construct on the Property, among other improvements, a _____ and all parking and service facilities related thereto (the "<u>Project</u>"). It is therefore specifically agreed that Purchaser's obligations hereunder are conditioned upon the satisfaction of each of the following conditions of this Paragraph 3(c). After the expiration of the Inspection Period, Purchaser's only conditions precedent to closing will be the Closing Conditions set forth in Paragraph 4 and Purchaser's Earnest Money will be non-refundable except as to such Closing Conditions. The conditions precedent are as follows:

    i. Purchaser obtaining, at Purchaser's expense, a title commitment, boundary line and topographical survey (the "<u>Survey</u>"), surveyor's report and surveyor's certificate, feasibility studies and any other appraisals, inspections, tests or studies desired by Purchaser showing to the satisfaction of Purchaser in its sole discretion that the Property is usable by Purchaser for the purpose of constructing and operating the Project. The Survey and any and all tests under this subparagraph must be completed by the end of the Inspection Period and any cancellation of the Agreement by Purchaser due to these items not being satisfactory must be done in writing prior to the expiration of the Inspection Period, otherwise they will be deemed to have been waived or satisfied.

    ii. Purchaser receiving confirmation that (a) all utility lines necessary for the construction and operation of the Project, including but not limited to water, telephone, storm sewer, natural gas and electricity lines, will be available at the boundaries of the Property and will be available, sufficient and satisfactory for Purchaser's use in connection with the construction and operation of the Project, and (b) Purchaser receiving confirmation that Purchaser will be able to obtain sewer taps and capacity sufficient to serve the needs of the Project, with all applicable governmental permits and authorizations, at a cost of no greater than _____ and No/100 Dollars ($_____) per unit to be developed in the Project.

   iii. Purchaser's receipt of a satisfactory report, prepared by an environmental engineer selected by Purchaser, with respect to the environmental condition of the Property and compliance of the Property with applicable environmental laws. Purchaser shall have a Phase One environmental examination of the Property prepared during the Inspection Period. Purchaser's environmental study of the Property may include, among other matters, studies of soil and groundwater contamination, asbestos, polychlorinated biphenyls (PCBs), lead in drinking water, lead based paint, radon gas, and wetlands.

   iv. Purchaser satisfying itself as to such other matters as Purchaser deems to be necessary or desirable for the construction and operation of the Project.

d. <u>Continuance of Agreement after Inspection Period</u>. Unless Purchaser notifies Seller in writing on or before the expiration of the Inspection Period that Purchaser has satisfied the contingencies set forth in subparagraph 3(c) above, then this Agreement shall terminate without further action of Purchaser, whereupon the Earnest Money shall be refunded to Purchaser by the Title Company except One Hundred ($100.00) Dollars of the Earnest Money which shall be paid to Seller in consideration of entering into this Agreement, and this Agreement shall be of no further force or effect with Purchaser and Seller having no further rights, obligations or liabilities hereunder except as specifically provided herein.

e. <u>Title and Survey</u>. Purchaser shall have until the expiration of the Inspection Period to examine the Survey of and title to the Property and to notify Seller of any objectionable matter or defect (a "<u>Title Objection</u>") which affects the marketability or insurability of the title to the Property or which adversely affects the use of the Property for the Project. In the event Seller is notified of any such Title Objections, Seller shall have fifteen (15) days from receipt of such written notice within which to notify Purchaser of Seller's intent to remove such Title Objections, failing which Purchaser shall have the option of either accepting the title as it is and waiving the Title Objections, or, terminating this Agreement and receiving a refund of the Earnest Money which shall immediately be returned to Purchaser by Title Company, and thereupon, Purchaser and Seller shall release (except as otherwise provided herein) one another of all further obligations under this Agreement. Seller shall, if title is found unmarketable, use diligent efforts to correct the defect(s) in the title within said fifteen (15) day period, including the bringing of any and all necessary suits. In addition to the foregoing, Seller shall be obligated to cure on or before the date of Closing (i) any voluntarily created encumbrances to secure the repayment of debt and (ii) any other Title Objections which can be satisfied by the expenditure of Seller's funds not to exceed $300,000.00.

f. <u>Seller's Deliveries</u>. Within five (5) days after the Effective Date, Seller shall deliver to Purchaser, to the extent not previously delivered by Seller to Purchaser and at Seller's expense, the Seller Deliverable Items (as hereinafter defined) described herein relating to the Property which are in the Seller's possession. At Purchaser's election, Seller shall permit Purchaser to have access to Seller's files in Seller's office to permit Purchaser to review such Seller Deliverable Items. As used herein, "<u>Seller Deliverable Items</u>" shall mean:

i. Copies of all tax bills for the Property;
ii. Copies of all environmental reports related to the Property;
iii. Copies of all surveys, plats, site plans and topographical maps related to the Property;
iv. Copies of all soils, geological and engineering reports related to the Property;
v. Information regarding zoning of the Property and other relevant land-use information, including any ongoing or recent rezoning applications;
vi. Copies of all utility agreements and reservations related to the Property;
vii. Copies of all title insurance policies and title exception documents for the Property;
viii. Copies of all leases of all or any part of the Property and other agreements relating to the use and operation of all or any part of the Property;
ix. Copies of plans for the other proposed improvements at the Property; and
x. Any other information, documents, plans or reports in Seller's possession, relating to the Property or the aforementioned items (i) through (ix).

4. <u>Closing</u>.

   a. <u>Closing Date</u>. The consummation of the purchase and sale of the Property contemplated under this Agreement (the "<u>Closing</u>") shall be held on or before the later of (i) the date which is _____ (____) days after the expiration of the Inspection Period, or (ii) _____ (____) days after Purchaser has obtained Final Legal Zoning of the Property (as defined in Paragraph 14), at an exact date and time designated by Purchaser to Seller in the offices of _____, or at such other location which may be designated by Purchaser (Purchaser will give Seller not less than five (5) days notice of such designation). Purchaser shall have the right to extend the Closing for an additional period of _____ (___) days upon written notice by Purchaser to Seller of such election given on or before five (5) days prior to the date for Closing. Seller shall deliver possession of the Property to Purchaser at Closing.

b. <u>Closing Conditions to be Satisfied Prior to Closing</u>. After the expiration of the Inspection Period, Purchaser's obligation to close shall at all times be conditioned upon the following (unless Purchaser waives such conditions; such conditions, the "<u>Closing Conditions</u>"):

   i. Seller delivering good and marketable fee simple title to the Property by limited or special warranty deed and all other items required to be delivered to Purchaser in accordance with the provisions of Paragraph 5 of this Agreement.

   ii. The truth and accuracy of Seller's warranties and representations in Paragraph 9 (Seller's Representations and Warranties) and 10 (Environmental, Health and Safety Matters) at the time of this Agreement, and the compliance by Seller with each and every covenant and agreement to be performed on its part in accordance with Paragraph 5 of this Agreement.

   iii. Seller promptly providing Purchaser with any written notices it receives from any governmental agency with respect to the Property.

   iv. Purchaser obtaining zoning of the Property for the Project as more particularly set forth in Paragraph 14 below to the extent necessary in accordance with all applicable rules, regulations, statutes and ordinances with such platting and/or zoning being validly and irrevocably granted on terms and conditions satisfactory to Purchaser, without qualification, except such qualification as shall be acceptable to Purchaser and no longer subject to appeal. Seller agrees at all times to fully cooperate with Purchaser's efforts to obtain such zoning of the Property and shall promptly execute upon request any and all documentation necessary to obtain such zoning of the Property.

v. Purchaser obtaining all site development permits and land disturbance permits and approvals, or local equivalents thereof, as required by all applicable governmental authorities permitting the development of the Project, and all such permits and approvals (and any conditions related thereto) shall be satisfactory to Purchaser in its sole discretion.

vi. No moratorium, restriction or other prohibition shall be imposed or threatened by any applicable governmental authority which shall restrict the development of the Project as a multifamily community or which shall restrict any utility company from providing service to the Project.

vii. No orders, suits, actions or proceedings shall have been instituted or threatened which would prohibit, restrict or limit the development of the Project.

Should Seller fail to satisfy (or Purchaser fail to waive) any one or more of the contingencies set forth in this subparagraph 4(b) by the date of Closing (if permissible under the terms of this Agreement), then Purchaser may terminate this Agreement by giving written notice to Seller, whereupon all Earnest Money shall be refunded to Purchaser except One Hundred ($100.00) Dollars of such Earnest Money which shall be paid to Seller in consideration of entering into this Agreement, and such termination shall be in addition to exercising any other remedy available to Purchaser hereunder.

c. <u>Closing Costs</u>. The premium for the issuance to Purchaser of a standard ALTA Form B Owner's Policy of Title Insurance for the Property in the amount of the Purchase

Price shall be paid by _____, the costs for preparation and update of the Survey (as hereinafter defined), Purchaser's attorney's fees, and all recording fees on recordable documents shall be paid by Purchaser. Seller shall be responsible for the payment of its own attorney's fees, any delinquent assessments due with respect to the Property, and all real estate transfer taxes.

    d. <u>Prorations at Closing</u>. All real property ad valorem taxes due with respect to the Property for the calendar year of the Closing shall be prorated (employing a 365-day year) between Purchaser and Seller as of the date of Closing based upon the most recently available property assessment. If the actual amount of such taxes is not known as of such date, either because bills for the period in question have not been issued or because such bills cover real property in addition to the Property, the proration at the Closing will be based on the most current and accurate billing information available. Should such proration not be based on the actual amount of the ad valorem taxes for the period in question and should such proration prove to be inaccurate upon receipt of the actual bills for the Property, then, to the extent such amount exceeds One Thousand and No/100 Dollars ($1,000.00), either Seller or Purchaser may demand at any time after the Closing Date a payment from the other party correcting such malapportionment. The provisions of this Paragraph shall survive the Closing.

5. <u>Conveyance of Title</u>.

    a. Seller shall convey good and marketable fee simple title to the Property to Purchaser at Closing pursuant to a recordable limited or special warranty deed (the "<u>Limited Warranty Deed</u>") duly executed, witnessed and authorized, free and clear of liens and encumbrances created by Seller and other Title Objections (as hereinafter defined) other than (i) Title Objections not cured by Seller and waived by

Purchaser and (ii) the lien for current ad valorem taxes not yet due and payable ((i) and (ii) hereinafter collectively referred to as "<u>Permitted Exceptions</u>"). For purposes of this Paragraph 5, "good and marketable fee simple title" shall mean fee simple ownership which is (a) free of all claims, liens and encumbrances of any kind or nature whatsoever, other than the Permitted Exceptions, and (b) insurable by Title Company at then current standard rates under the standard form of ALTA owner's policy of title insurance (ALTA Form B 1992), with the standard printed exceptions therein deleted, and without exceptions or exclusions from coverage other than for the Permitted Exceptions. The legal description to be incorporated into the Limited Warranty Deed shall be prepared utilizing common boundaries of the legal description of the Property attached as <u>Exhibit "A"</u>. If the common boundaries of the legal description of the Property, as depicted on the Survey, are not the same as the legal description attached to this Agreement, Seller will, at Closing, execute and deliver to Purchaser a recordable Quitclaim Deed duly executed, witnessed and notarized containing a legal description of the Property prepared from the Survey.

b. Seller shall deliver to purchaser at Closing such evidence as purchaser's counsel and/or the Title Company may reasonably require as to the authority of the person or persons executing documents on behalf of the Seller.

c. Seller shall execute and deliver to Purchaser at Closing such additional documents as shall be reasonably required to consummate the transaction expressly contemplated in this Agreement.

d. Seller shall deliver to Purchaser and the Title Company at Closing an affidavit acceptable to Purchaser and the Title Company stating that (i) there have been no improvements, additions, alterations, repairs or any changes of any kind whatsoever made to the Property by Seller during the last one hundred (100) days immediately preceding Closing, or if there have been any such improvements or repairs, that all lienors or potential lienors in connection with such improvements or repairs have been paid in full; (ii) that Seller is not a "foreign person" as that term is defined in the I.R.C., Section 1445 (F) (3), nor is the sale of the Property subject to any withholding requirements imposed by the Internal Revenue Code, including, but not limited to, Section 1445 thereof, or in the event any such withholdings are required, then Seller shall withhold such amounts from the Purchase Price as required by law; (iii) no legal proceedings are pending or to Seller's knowledge threatened against Seller which could affect Seller's title to the Property or right or power of Seller to convey the Property to Purchaser in accordance with this Agreement; and (iv) such other matters as Purchaser's title insurer may reasonably require in order to insure Purchaser's good and marketable fee simple title to the Property.

6. Casualty and Condemnation. In the event, at any time between the making of this Agreement and Closing, all or any material portion of the Property is condemned by any legally constituted authority for any public use or purpose then Purchaser may elect to either: (i) terminate this Agreement, in which event all Earnest Money paid by Purchaser shall be immediately refunded to Purchaser, and neither Purchaser nor Seller shall have any further liabilities, obligations or rights with regard to this Agreement; or (ii) consummate the purchase of the Property and collect all proceeds from any condemnation and have the terms of this Agreement remain in full force and effect and binding on the parties hereto with no reduction in the Purchase Price. In the event of a condemnation in which Purchaser does not elect to terminate this Agreement, then Seller shall on Closing pay any and all condemnation awards and compensation then received by Seller to Purchaser. In addition, Seller shall assign to Purchaser all rights

and claims of Seller with respect to payment and compensation on account at such taking. In the event of a condemnation in which Purchaser does not elect to terminate this Agreement pursuant to the foregoing terms, then the term "Property" as used herein shall thereafter refer to the Property less and except any portion thereof taken by such condemnation.

Seller shall notify Purchaser immediately upon Seller's receiving notice of the occurrence or existence of any condemnation or threat of condemnation affecting the Property and, at the same time, shall provide Purchaser with such information with respect thereto as is in Seller's possession in order to aid Purchaser in making, on an informed basis, the election between the alternatives provided by clauses (i) and (ii) above in this Paragraph 6. Notwithstanding anything in this Agreement to the contrary, Purchaser shall have fifteen (15) days after Purchaser receives such information from Seller within which to elect between such alternatives, and, accordingly, the Closing Date shall be postponed, if and to the extent necessary, to allow Purchaser such a fifteen (15) day period in which to make the election under this Paragraph 6.

7. <u>Agreement Assignable by Purchaser.</u> This Agreement may be assigned or transferred by Purchaser to an affiliate of Purchaser without Seller's consent or approval, so long as Purchaser remains liable for the performance of the obligations hereunder.

8. <u>Survival of Closing.</u> All warranties, covenants and representations made herein by either Seller or Purchaser shall survive Closing for a period of twelve (12) months.

9. <u>Seller's Representations and Warranties.</u> Seller represents, warrants and covenants to Purchaser that:

   a. Seller has complete and full authority to execute this Agreement and to convey to Purchaser title to the Property in accordance with Paragraph 5 of this Agreement.

b. Seller has not received any written notice of any possible future improvements that might create an assessment against any part of the Property.

c. Seller has no knowledge of nor has Seller received any written notice of any pending or threatened taking or condemnation of the Property or any portion thereof.

d. To the knowledge of Seller, no assessments have been made against any portion of the Property which are unpaid (except ad valorem taxes for the current year). Seller shall notify Purchaser upon learning of any such assessments.

e. There are no leases or occupancy agreements currently affecting any portion of the Property and exclusive possession of the Property shall be delivered by Seller to Purchaser at Closing free of the rights or claims of any tenants, occupants or other parties in possession of or having or claiming any right to possession or use of the Property under, by or through the rights of Seller whether such rights or claims are through lease, easement, license or otherwise.

f. No right-of-first refusal or similar agreement exists in connection with the Property which would in any way interfere with Seller's ability to sell the Property.

g. Neither the entering into of this Agreement nor the consummation of the transaction contemplated hereby will constitute or result in a violation or breach by Seller of any judgment, order, writ, injunction or decree issued against or imposed upon it. There is no action, suit, proceeding or investigation pending against Seller which would become a cloud on the title to the Property or any portion thereof or which questions the validity or enforceability of the transaction contemplated by this Agreement or any action taken pursuant hereto in any court or before or by any federal, district, county, or municipal department, commission, board, bureau, agency or other governmental instrumentality.

h. Seller has no knowledge of, nor has Seller received any written notice of, any actual or threatened action, litigation, or proceeding by any organization, person, individual or governmental agency (including governmental actions under condemnation authority or proceedings similar thereto) against the Property or Seller, nor has any such organization, person, individual or governmental agency communicated to Seller in writing anything which Seller believes to be a threat of any such action, litigation or proceeding.

i. Seller has not received actual, written notice of any violations of law, municipal or county ordinances, or other legal requirements with respect to the Property.

10. <u>Environmental, Health and Safety Matters.</u>

a. Seller possesses, and is in full compliance with, any permits, licenses and government authorizations, required with respect to the Property and has filed any notices that are required under local, state and federal laws relating to protection of the environment, pollution control, product registration and Hazardous Materials (the "<u>Environmental Laws</u>").

b. To its knowledge, Seller is not subject to any claim, obligation, liability, loss, damage or expense of whatever kind or nature, contingent or otherwise, incurred or imposed or based upon any provision of any Environmental Law or arising out of any act or omission of Seller, or Seller's employees, agents or representatives or arising out of the ownership, use, control or operation by Seller of any facility, site, area or property from which any

Hazardous Materials were released into the environment (the term "release" meaning any spilling, leaking, pumping, pouring, emitting, emptying, discharging, injecting, escaping, leaching, dumping or disposing into the environment, and the term "environment" meaning any surface or ground water, drinking water supply, soil, surface or subsurface strata or medium, or the ambient air);

c. Seller has no actual knowledge that the Property, improvements or equipment located on the Property contain any asbestos, PCBs, underground storage tanks, open or closed pits, dumps or other containers on or under any such assets; and

d. Seller has not imported any Hazardous Materials onto the Property.

e. "Hazardous Materials" means any waste, pollutant, contaminant, hazardous substance, toxic, ignitable, reactive or corrosive substance, hazardous waste, special waste, industrial substance, by-product, process intermediate product or waste, petroleum or petroleum-derived substance or waste, chemical liquids or solids, liquid or gaseous products, or any constituent of any such substance or waste, the use, handling or disposal of which by Seller is in any way governed by or subject to any applicable Environmental Law."

11. <u>Notices</u>. All notices, requests, demands or other communications hereunder shall be in writing and deemed given when delivered personally, when telefaxed or sent via a nationally recognized overnight courier service, or on the day said communication is deposited in the U.S. mail, by registered or certified mail, return receipt requested, postage prepaid, addressed as follows:

If to Seller: _____

_____

_____

FAX No. _____

If to Purchaser: _____

_____

_____

FAX No. _____

or to such other address as the parties may from time to time designate by notice in writing to the other parties.

12. <u>Amendment</u>. Neither this Agreement nor any provision hereof may be changed, amended, modified, waived or discharged orally or by any course of dealing, but only by an instrument in writing signed by the party against which enforcement of the change, amendment, modification, waiver or discharge is sought.

13. <u>Legal Fees</u>. In the event legal action is instituted by any of the parties to enforce the terms of this Agreement or arising out of the execution of this Agreement, the prevailing party will be entitled to receive from the other party or parties reasonable attorney's fees to be determined by the court in which the action is brought.

14. <u>Final Legal Zoning</u>. Purchaser shall diligently submit an application to _____[City/County] for the rezoning of the Property to permit development of the Project and Purchaser's intended use (the "<u>Application</u>"). Assuming that the Application is approved, such approval, together with the expiration of any applicable appeal period with respect to the approval shall be considered the "<u>Final Legal Zoning</u>" of the Property. If Purchaser is unable to obtain the Final Legal Zoning for the Property after diligent efforts by Purchaser, then this Agreement may be terminated by Purchaser by giving written notice to Seller. Upon such termination, all Earnest Money shall be promptly returned to

Purchaser and this Agreement shall be null and void and of no further force and effect.

15. <u>Brokers</u>. Each party represents and warrants to the other that no real estate broker or agent other than _____ (the "<u>Broker</u>") are instrumental in the procurement of this Agreement. At Closing, Seller shall pay to Broker a brokerage fee pursuant to a separate agreement. Additionally, Purchaser and Seller represent and warrant that no other real estate commission or compensation shall be payable by such party with respect to the procurement and execution of this Agreement or the sale of the Property contemplated hereby. Each party shall indemnify and save the other party wholly harmless against any loss, cost, or other expense, including reasonable attorney's fees, that may be incurred by such other party by reason of any breach of the foregoing warranties.

16. <u>Default</u>. In the event the purchase and sale is not consummated because of the inability, failure or refusal, for whatever reason whatsoever, by Seller to convey the Property in accordance with the terms and conditions provided herein, or because of other fault of Seller, all Earnest Money and other sums paid in connection with this Agreement shall be returned by Title Company and Seller to Purchaser, without prejudice to any other legal or equitable right or remedy of Purchaser against Seller including, but not limited to, specific performance and damages. In the event the purchase and sale is not consummated because of the default of Purchaser, then Title Company shall deliver the Earnest Money to Seller, and Seller shall retain Earnest Money (and any non-refundable fees, if any, already paid), as full, complete and final liquidated damages. Seller and Purchaser hereby agree that it would be impossible to ascertain the damages accruing to Seller as a result of a default by Purchaser under this Agreement. The payment of said liquidated damages therefore shall constitute Seller's sole remedy against Purchaser and shall be in lieu of the exercise by Seller of any other legal or equitable right or remedy which Seller may have against Purchaser as a result of Purchaser's default.

17. Applicable Law. This Agreement shall be governed by and construed and enforced in accordance with the laws of the State of _____.

18. Waiver. Failure of either Purchaser or Seller to exercise any right given hereunder or to insist upon strict compliance with regard to any term, condition or covenant specified herein, shall not constitute a waiver of Purchaser's or Seller's right to exercise such right or to demand strict compliance with any term, condition or covenant under this Agreement.

19. Counterparts. This Agreement may be executed in several counterparts, each of which may be deemed an original, and all of such counterparts together shall constitute one and the same Agreement.

20. Captions. All captions, headings, paragraph and subparagraph numbers and letters are solely for reference purposes and shall not be deemed to be supplementing, limiting, or otherwise varying the text of this Agreement.

21. Severability. The invalidity or enforceability of a particular provision of this Agreement shall not affect the other provisions hereof, and this Agreement shall be construed in all respects as if such invalid or unenforceable provision were omitted.

22. Entire Agreement. Time is of the essence of this Agreement. This Agreement constitutes the sole and entire agreement of the parties and is binding upon Seller and Purchaser, their heirs, successors, legal representatives and assigns.

23. Confidentiality. Except as otherwise provided herein, it is agreed that the existence and the terms and conditions of this Agreement shall be kept confidential by Seller and Purchaser, and not disclosed to third-parties. Notwithstanding the confidentiality provisions herein, Seller or Purchaser may disclose the existence and/or contents of this Agreement: (i) as and only to the extent

required by law; (ii) as necessary to seek appropriate advice from professional advisors, including tax preparers, bank personnel, business advisors, legal advisors, lenders, and financial advisors; (iii) as necessary to enforce the terms of this Agreement, or (iv) if the information is already a matter of public record or generally known to the public other than as a result of an act or omission by the party seeking to disclose such information. Each of Seller and Purchaser shall require third parties (such as management companies and contractors) to abide by comparable confidentiality provisions with respect to the terms and conditions of the Agreement.

24. <u>Exclusivity</u>. During the term of this Agreement, Purchaser and Seller hereby acknowledge and agree that Purchaser shall have the sole and exclusive right to purchase the Property and Seller shall not commence, undertake or continue any negotiations with any other party concerning the sale of the Property.

25. <u>Date of Agreement</u>. The "<u>Effective Date</u>" of this Agreement shall be the date each of Purchaser and Seller has executed this Agreement and the date of receipt of the fully executed Agreement by each party. Purchaser and Seller hereby agree that upon execution and delivery of the Agreement, Seller and Purchaser shall confirm in writing the Effective Date of the Agreement. In the event that any applicable date under this Agreement falls on a Saturday, Sunday or holiday recognized by the state in which the Property is located such date shall be extended to the next applicable business day.

IN WITNESS WHEREOF, the parties have caused this Agreement to be executed on the respective dates written below.

SELLER:

Name: _____
Title: _____

Date: _____

PURCHASER:

Name: _____
Title: _____

Date: _____

Courtesy of Kwame A. Benjamin, Seyfarth Shaw LLP

APPENDIX P
SAMPLE CLOSING CHECKLIST

Purchase of Two Properties Portfolio with Finance with CRE Loan
(exclusive of CRE loan closing checklist requirements)

	Acquisition of "ABC Company" Portfolio	
PROPERTIES:	FAR AWAY, TX Purchase Price: $_____ Loan: $_____	NEVERLAND, NV Purchase Price: $_____ Loan: $_____
BUYERS:	XXX LLC	YYY LLC
SELLER:	ABC Company	
COUNSEL FOR SELLER:	Seller Attorney _____ _____ Attn: _____ Tele: _____ Fax: _____ Email: _____	

	Responsible Party	Status/Comments
CLOSING DOCUMENTS – ABC Company Portfolio Acquisition Neverland: Purchase Price: $ _____ Loan Amount: $ _____ Far Away: Purchase Price: $ _____ Loan Amount: $ _____		
1. Purchase & Sale Agreement a. First Amendment		
2. Purchaser's Approval Notice		
3. Purchaser's Direction to Seller to Convey to "Far Away" and "Neverland" Entities		

4. Deeds
   a. Far Away, TX
   b. Neverland, NV		

5. State of Nevada Declaration of Value Form		

6.	Bill of Sale
	  a. Far Away, TX
	  b. Neverland, NV				

7.	Assignment of Leases
	  a. Far Away, TX
	  b. Neverland, NV				

8.	Assignment and Assumption of Contracts and Intangibles
	  a. Far Away, TX
	  b. Neverland, NV				

9.	Tenant Notice Letter
	  a. Far Away, TX
	  b. Neverland, NV				

10.	GSA Statement of Lease
	  a. Far Away, TX
	  b. Neverland, NV				

11.	GSA Novation Agreement a. Far Away, TX b. Neverland, NV					
12.	GSA Approval of Sale					
13.	FIRPTA Form 8288-B and Withholding Escrow Agreement a. Far Away, TX b. Neverland, NV					
14.	Owner's Title Affidavits a. Far Away, TX b. Neverland, NV					
15.	Seller's Certificate a. Far Away, TX b. Neverland, NV					
16.	Purchaser's Certificate a. Far Away, TX b. Neverland, NV					

17.	Settlement Statement / Closing Statement
	  a. Far Away, TX
	  b. Neverland, NV			

18.	Release of Declaration
	  a. Far Away, TX
	  b. Neverland, NV			

19.	Seller's Sched. B Title Requirements a. Entity good standing & authority			
20.	Purchaser's Escrow Instruction Letter(s)			
	TITLE / SURVEY / MISCELLANEOUS			

21.	Title Commitments
	  a. Far Away, TX
	  b. Neverland, NV			

22.	Pro-Forma Title Policies
	  a. Far Away, TX
	  b. Neverland, NV			

23.	Final ALTA/ACSM Land Title Surveys a. Far Away, TX b. Neverland, NV		
24.	Estoppel Certificate		
25.	CRE Requirements & Loan Documents		
	ORGANIZATIONAL DOCUMENTS		
1.	Group XY LLC <u>Sole member of:</u> XXX LLC YYY LLC		
	(i) Certificate of Formation		
	(ii) Qualification to do Business in {STATE}		
	(iii) Operating Agreement		
	(iv) Good Standing Certificate		
	(v) Independent Manager Service Agreement		

	(vi) Tax Identification Number		
2.	XXX LLC		
	(i) Certificate of Formation		
	(ii) Qualification to do Business in {STATE}		
	(iii) Operating Agreement		
	(iv) Good Standing Certificate		
	(v) Tax Identification Number		
3.	YYY LLC		
	(i) Certificate of Formation		
	(ii) Name Registration		
	(iii) Qualification to do Business in {STATE}		
	(iv) Operating Agreement		
	(v) Good Standing Certificate		

(vi) Tax Identification Number

Legal Opinion Firms

State Opinion Counsel

_____
_____
_____

Attn: _____
Tele: _____
Fax: _____
Email: _____

State Opinion Counsel

_____
_____
_____

Attn: _____
Tele: _____
Fax: _____
Email: _____

Lender's Counsel

_____
_____
_____

Attn: _____
Tele: _____
Fax: _____
Email: _____

State Non-Consolidation Opinion:

_____
_____
_____

Attn: _____
Tele: _____
Fax: _____
Email: _____

Purchase of Property

_____ (Purchaser)	_____ (Purchaser's Counsel)
Attn: _____ Tele: _____ Fax: _____ Email: _____	Attn: _____ Tele: _____ Fax: _____ Email: _____
_____ (Seller)	_____ (Seller's Counsel)
Attn: _____ Tele: _____ Fax: _____ Email: _____	Attn: _____ Tele: _____ Fax: _____ Email: _____

Courtesy of Kwame A. Benjamin, Seyfarth Shaw LLP